G000093149

# HOW I WON
# MY WAR

# HOW I WON
# MY WAR

## From Discrimination
## To Admiration

CHARLY NGOUH

*"There is no education like adversity"*

- BENJAMIN DISRAELI

# CONTENTS

# PREFACE

Hello... I am Charly Ngouh (pronunciation: *goo*)! My name, as you can see, is a combination of a very western first name and an authentic African tribe surname. I have been living in the United Kingdom for eighteen years up to the point of writing this third edition of my book and the correct pronunciation of my surname has been a struggle for most people I have come in contact with.

I want to feel at home with you, my reader, and so let me show you how to say my name properly. It is simply pronounced goo like good, but without the 'd' and the 'n' is silent.

Cameroon, the country of my birth, is located in Central Africa and surrounded by Nigeria to west, Chad and the Central African Republic to the east, Gabon, Congo (Brazzaville) and Equatorial Guinea to the south. Because of its unique history, it is the only African country that has French and English in its constitution as official languages. It is mostly known for the unforgettable performance of its national football team at the World Cup in Italy in 1990. Roger Milla is its most famous player.

My parents were very young when they agreed to enter an arranged marriage and knew very little about each other at the beginning. Their relationship turned out later to be an extremely painful roller-coaster ride which presented me, their first child, with a dilemma that I struggled with throughout my teenage years. I was faced with difficult choices and did my best to accommodate both my parents who, despite living under the same roof, seemed to be in different worlds.

I first discovered the West in 1997. I was seventeen and as a representative of my father's company, I visited Germany to meet with partners. During my visit, I went to great lengths to make myself likeable and it paid off. I was invited to spend the summer months with my german friends two years later. Those visits enabled me to learn and practice German, a language in which I am now fluent.

In 2001, after a failed business venture in the Czech Republic, I moved to the United Kingdom to study law at a university. After my father pulled the plug on the funding of my education, I joined the British Army as a Foreign and Commonwealth soldier. I served in the British Armed Forces for nearly five years. During my service, I went on a six months operational tour of duty in Iraq in 2006 from Germany where I was stationed. I left the Army and returned to civilian life in April 2008.

This book is about the challenges I faced as an older child in a dysfunctional family and the emotional pain caused by my tireless endeavour to please and keep both my parents together. It will touch on my quest to make something unique out of my life from a very young age and my determination to enjoy a productive and fulfilling existence in the United Kingdom.

Without being critical of the British Armed Forces, this book will examine the difficulties and struggles of my journey as a soldier in a setting that brings together varied cultures without taking their differences into account.

This book does not simply narrate what happened to a former soldier who believes that his life experiences are worthy of your attention. It brings to you a story that is real, vibrant and important to you - a human story. You will be able to draw out something from it that you will connect with and use it to good effect in your life.

This is the story of an immigrant who simply wanted to live in peace, joy and happiness and also to get on with others and his own life. After two years of struggle and difficulty, fighting to be granted the right to enjoy freedom in the United Kingdom as a lawful citizen, I began questioning myself.

It occurred to me that my priorities might not be in the right order. As a result of this introspection, my ambition to make a lot of money was replaced by the will to help a lot of people. This was a decision that I came to after going through personal development and self improvement. I realised that by being able to give others value in terms of ideas, support and encouragement, I got back respect, attention and appreciation.

As you can tell from its title, this book is about me fighting my wars; which is simply another way of explaining my life's challenges. The situations that I faced may be different to the ones in your life right now, but the effects I had were the same: pain, frustration, anger, helplessness, hopelessness, disillusion...

Whether it is in your job, in your family or in your quest for self-discovery, I trust that you will gain from my experiences, my positive attitude and my determination in the face of adversity. As a result, you will be better equipped to deal with your own personal wars. You will also benefit by following the way I turned my bad judgements and poor decisions into stepping stones to uncover what I believe to be my life purpose; which is to positively impact the lives of others.

Writing a book had been on my mind for many years, but like most people, I kept putting it off until early 2015 when I sat down, drew up a plan of action and acted on it immediately. I hope that you will be inspired to the point of taking the same steps after reading my story. I know that you will then make the world a better place by sharing your own journey.

My story is unique of its kind. I am sure that yours is too. My hope is that after reading this book, you will take a journey within and unlock the part of you that will help you live a more fulfilled life. It really doesn't matter who you are or what you do, what your background is or what language you speak, it is good to share our personal stories with others to enrich their lives. You are never too old to learn and never too young to teach.

What you are about to read is the story of my life, my childhood, my relationship with my parents, how I came and settled in the United Kingdom, my time in the British Army, my life after the Army, what my ambitions are and how I intend to impact the world; which I hope will inspire you as well.

As you read my story, there will be times when you will feel sorry for me. Please don't. There will also be times when you will feel that I deserved all the horrible results in my life and I agree with you.

So, welcome to my world and let's start from the day it all began - March 15, 1980.

# CHAPTER ONE

# The Early Days

I have a scar at the back of my head just behind my left ear. I always stress its presence to the barbers when I go for a haircut. Although it isn't painful, it is quite prominent and has been there since my birth. I never miss any opportunity to share the details surrounding its occurrence when people ask me about it. The way I explain is that I was a big baby who could not have been brought into this world without complications.

To those who insist on knowing more, I go a little further to explain that my mother's pelvis was too narrow for a normal birth and doctors had to use forceps to pull me out. The instruments used for the extraction were rudimentary and caused an injury that healed over time and left a scar for life. That is what I said and it was all I knew until it turned out the story of my birth was a lot more dramatic as I discovered after a conversation with my mother in preparation for the writing of this book.

Charlotte gave me the chilling details of a process that began four days before I was born.

On the 11th of March 1980 at the age of seventeen and a half, she was pregnant for the second time after a miscarriage a few months earlier. She was not feeling well and hadn't eaten properly for days. She vomited every time she attempted to swallow anything and was feeling dizzy and light-headed as her unborn child was kicking in her belly on that hot Tuesday morning.

She was home by herself. Jean, her twenty-four year old husband and government official, was away on duty for a few days. There was no way of contacting him immediately as no phones were available at the time. The only way to make him aware of his young wife's discomfort was to go physically to his work place and leave a message that would then be passed onto him. A process that could take a couple of days. Based on the previous medical visit, the delivery wasn't due for another two weeks. But it seemed that the baby had made other plans.

The community within which Charlotte and Jean lived quickly rallied around the teenage mother-to-be for the much needed support. After a quick assessment of the situation by some experienced mothers in that highly polluted neighbourhood, the decision was made to rush the pain stricken young woman to the maternity ward of the Local General Hospital.

She was fatigued, overwhelmed and scared that this pregnancy would end like the one before. She really had no reason to worry because the pregnancy had gone well up to that point. But the fact that it might be an early birth made her extremely uneasy. Her waters broke later that day.

The delivery process began with a lot of pain. She pushed and pushed hard, then harder some more. It turned out during the early stages of delivery that her pelvis was too small for her big-headed baby boy. Caesarian was considered, but the nurses realised that such an attempt could endanger the life of the baby and/or the mother. The pain was excruciating as she attempted to deliver naturally over a few hours.

The following day, Charlotte and the nurses waited patiently for a miracle to happen as she tried her best to handle her internal aches. Still on the delivery bed, she was sweating a lot and with a dusty fan blowing hot air from the ceiling, the labour process took another two days and was still fruitless. Nurses realised that her organs could be irreversibly damaged if the delivery was forced. Patience and observation seemed to be sensible options.

Understandably restless at night, she caught some sleep every now and then when her pains subsided. In the meantime, Jean had received the news and made his way back to be by the side of his wife in the early hours on Friday, three full days after she had been admitted at the hospital. After a full debrief by the medical staff, a concerted decision was made to wait a little while longer before taking any drastic measures.

The next day, nurses decided that something had to be done quickly. A more senior doctor was assigned as the urgency grew. The decision was made, with the consent of both parents, to pull the baby out using the forceps at hand. Charlotte had lost too much blood in the process up to that point that It became apparent that her life had to be prioritised over that of the unborn child.

The rudimentary medical materials were awful but options were limited after an ordeal that had gone on for too long. The nurses and the specialist doctor coordinated the delivery and the desperate mother gave all she had. She pushed whilst the doctor pinched the baby's head with the forceps and pulled him out.

That was the process that led to me coming into this world on Saturday the 15th of March 1980.

I did not cry and was not even breathing at first. I was immediately taken away to the premature babies department and placed in an incubator as I urgently needed oxygen. In the meantime, my mother was pale and too worn out to even ask to see me. My father stayed around as he had taken leave from work. He was kept in tune with the progress of his first child who eventually survived the ordeal and started breathing normally after a few hours.

On Monday, March 17th, 1980, the highly emotion-charged moment came when I was handed over to my mother. She was seeing me for the first time, two days after my birth. She held me in her trembling arms and so began a mother-son relationship that would be tested over the months and years to come.

The delivery process had caused a lot of physical injuries and exhaustion to Charlotte and as a result, she needed some stitching done and monitoring for another two weeks after the lengthy ordeal. I had some serious damage too. As the doctor and nurses pulled me out using the rusted instruments, they peeled off the soft skin at the back of my head causing an open injury that made looking after me a real challenge.

The injury got worse over a considerable period of time after my birth and had to be attended to twice daily for about three months. My father being away most of the time on duty, my care was the responsibility of my mother alone; even-though she did get some sporadic support from extended family members. From what she told me recently, I was a non-stop-crying and always-hungry baby. Her motherly duties took a toll on her for a while in the early stages. But eventually, she got used to the long sleepless nights in her mosquito-infested small bedroom.

Her own injuries healed well over the years and she had six other children over a period of 25 years, all natural births. My injury also healed gradually over the ensuing months and years but left the scar that would later become a good conversation starter for me. It also earned me a lot of sympathy from those who noticed it.

My parents did not meet each other in a conventional way; it was not a boy meets girl kind of union. It was rather a girl is given to a man kind of situation. Jean was a young, hard working single man with a bright future ahead of him as a civil servant. Having a wife was perceived as a sign of maturity, an undeniable expression of manhood. Charlotte, being an orphan, was considered a burden by her older siblings. As far as they were concerned, letting her go to share her young life with an older man was a relief on them. She had never met her husband-to-be before and did not really understand what she was getting herself into. Fortunately, he was a good man, a man with integrity and good family values.

We had very little at home, but it didn't matter because happiness was always in the air. We had no television and my friends and I spent all of our spare time playing hide and seek around mango trees and wooden houses. At lunch time, regardless of which house we found ourselves in, the mother in that home would put food in one or two plates and place them in one corner. We would gather around the plates and start a spontaneous eating competition. Some of us with running noses would use the left hand to clean up with while eating with the right unwashed hand.

I took too many risks as a child. I came home all the time with new injuries caused by my attempts to either jump higher in the sand, run in the woods with no shoes on and causing wounds all over my skinny frame. Sometimes, I swam in stagnant ponds and drank their infested waters. Then I would get sick and Daddy would take care of me. My father was my hero.

Every Sunday, without fail, he gathered me and my brothers, lined us up in front of him and meticulously cut our finger nails. Every morning during the week he got up very early and his way to let us know was to turn his small two batteries radio on and turn the volume right up. My mother got us ready and Daddy took us to school. We always had sufficient raw food at home ready to be cooked. There was usually a bag of rice and a jug of palm oil in one corner of the house, some yams, potatoes or plantains in another. With no electricity and no running water, we lived in what could best be described as a wooden hut. Yet, life was simply amazing.

In 1985, at the age of five, my dad took me for a ride on his old bike.

I sat at the back and held him around his waist and with no helmet on for protection, we rode to the Douala International Airport (DLA) to visit some of his friends who worked there. When we got to our destination, my father was like a famous person, everyone we met knew his name. I was astonished when we entered the airport's main hall. I had never been there before and did not know that the world was more than the close-knit community in which I was growing up.

The main hall of the airport was big with a lot of paintings on its walls. There were nicely dressed people everywhere. Some had luggage of various shapes and colours, others were just walking around and admiring a very unusual environment. The air inside was slightly cold and smelt a mixture of different perfumes. I was very excited to be in a world completely different to the one I was used to.

My Dad bought me an ice-cream. I hadn't had anything like that before. It was very sweet and tasted like the chocolate that Mummy had bought my brother and me the Christmas before. As I was looking around, admiring people and taking in the sounds and colours of the immense hall, I noticed a very strange looking man. He was tall, wearing a nice blue pair of trousers with a clean jacket with lots of shiny things on it. He had a funny hat. His sunglasses looked like the one my best friend's father had. There was something very unusual about this tall man who, to me, stood out from the crowd. His skin colour was white.

In my community, there was a woman who had the same skin colour, but unlike the man at the airport whose hair was black, hers was white. We called her Mama Albino. She was an Albino woman. I didn't understand why two people with the same skin colour would have different hair colours. I kept looking at him and as he got closer to me, he smiled and I noticed that he had clean white teeth.

Mama Albino's teeth were not white, instead, they were kind of yellowish. That discovery made the mystery ever more complex. But I was too busy savouring my ice-cream that I could not be distracted for too long. A short while after, I spotted more of those white-skinned people around. Two women in very clean clothes were walking in the same direction as the tall man with the hat. I had to find out more.

So, I asked my Dad: "Papa, who are these people and where do they come from?"

My Dad smiled and told me: "Those are white people from Europe."

I was seeing white people for the first time at the age of five and I loved the way they looked. I wanted to know more about these strange looking people so I asked my Dad questions:

"So where is Europe?" I asked.

"Very far away from here", he answered.

"Can you take me there on the bike?" I inquired.

"No, it is too far from here", he said.

"What about a taxi?" I asked.

"It is too far and to go there, you need to enter that big machine" he concluded pointing at an aeroplane.

He took me to a large glass window, held me by the hip and lifted my tiny frame slightly above his head. Through the windows, I could see two big planes parked on the tarmac. One was the German Lufthansa and the other was a British Airways plane.

"Wow!! white people have very nice things", I told my dad.

After a few more minutes of me gazing at the planes with envy, he held my hand and took me to the British Airways office. When we got there, one of the white women picked me up and sat me on her lap. Her hair was black and dropping on both shoulders. Her eyes were very beautiful and a sweet smell came out of her mouth as she spoke to me in French with an accent that I had never heard before.

There was a box of candy in the corner of her desk and she invited me to grab a handful. I didn't want to leave that office. Two big machines were standing on both sides of the large desk she shared with her colleague. I later found out that those white boxes with cases of buttons were computers. After a little while, my Dad persuaded me to leave with him by promising that we would be back the following weekend.

On the way home that day, my father added a condition to his promise. He said that we would only be back if I stopped injuring myself. He really couldn't have come up with a better incentive to keep me straight. The next Saturday, we were back again and I kept returning to that airport most weekends in my teenage years. I fell in love with two things during that initial visit: Airports and white people. I kept thinking that a day would come when I will get on one of those planes to go where white people came from.

In 1990, at the age of ten, I was forced to work in my Uncle's farms during the school holidays. I was very reluctant to do that. It was hard work, too hard for me at that age and it also took me away from my friends with whom I enjoyed playing.

But my mother obliged me to do everything that her older brother required of me. I worked so hard that I got scratches on my arms and feet and sometimes on my face from manually collecting and assembling crops for long hours every day. My Uncle was tight- fisted. I got nothing in exchange for my work and he was abusive in his language when things did not go his way. When I made the slightest of mistakes, he cussed and told me that I was lazy and would never amount to anything in my life. I was ten years old.

His excuse for using me in his farms with no reward was that he had taken care of my mother when she was a little girl and so it was fair that her offspring should work for him free of charge. I became the collateral victim of an unwritten family tradition.

His wife, now deceased, was a really difficult woman to be around. She was physically imposing and had the nastiest of looks at times. She was always looking for quick fixes and easy gains at the expense of everybody else around her. She was, however, very protective of her own children. I spent a lot of my time in the company of this couple and they, literally, robbed me of my childhood in the early years of my life.

My mother also forced my younger brother Parfait and I to go to church. She made sure we attended Bible study at the local Catholic church every Saturday afternoon. We would go to Bible study, but I would always find a way to skive most of the time. I was not into the Bible, the Church, God - none of that really interested me.

Parfait, on the contrary, loved it. He was so interested that he became a devout Christian. I can't explain why, but it just wasn't for me. Nobody discouraged or prevented me from becoming a church-goer. I just didn' t want to be part of any religion from the outset and my mother's authority did nothing to change that.

I also had a problem that my mother thought could be resolved only if I was more involved with the church. I bed wetted quite a lot. I would get up almost every morning soaking wet from urinating in bed multiple times during the night. And because I sometimes shared the bed with one or two cousins, they would get wet because of me. It was a really tricky situation, not just for me but also for my parents who could not send me to an Uncle or an Aunty for a couple of days in a row without hearing the embarrassing news. I was beaten most of the time and shamed because of a condition that I could not control. It stopped around the age of eleven or twelve.

My early teenage years were quite eventful. As a first born, I started to feel the weight of the responsibility of such a position. My mother was very hard on me and although it didn't feel like it at the time, I now believe that it was justified. After all, she almost lost her life in the process of bringing me into this world.

She did all she could to keep me straight and being a bit of a mischievous child, I can honestly say that I would have strayed if she had not been as rigorous as she was. My siblings did not get the same treatment. Mummy wanted me to clear the path for them to follow. I was very scared of her punishments when I did something wrong.

One day, she came home late at night and we were already asleep. She burst into the bedroom that I shared with my brother, found us laying under the duvet and started to beat me really hard with an umbrella. I am not sure what I did wrong, but the pain and memory of that night remained with me for months. I had done something she disapproved of for sure but I doubted that all of the beating was needed. But again she risked her life to have me and I guess it was the only method she knew of to keep me on the right track.

In contrast, my father was very diplomatic. He always looked at the positive side of all situations and never raised his voice at me, my siblings or my mother. He was gentle, compassionate, disarmingly understanding and a true family man.

In 1992, at twelve years old, all the weight I had been carrying around until then had gone and my upper body had started to develop and show some real manly muscles. However, my legs remained skinny. During that time and for reasons unbeknown to me, one of my best friends turned on me. He was violent and rejoiced at me being in pain. He hit and punched me just for fun. I never tried to defend myself. I was scared of everyone and very fearful as a result of my mother's regular beatings and my Uncle's horrendous treatment. What was even worse for me was that I thought I deserved the pain and blamed myself for all the hurt that I was subjected to.

There came a point when I got so sick and tired of being bullied and pushed around by people of the same age. I joined a martial art club and started kickboxing lessons. But my Dad had different ideas. He wanted me to play football. We had just witnessed the amazing performance of Cameroon at the World Cup in 1990. Daddy hoped that his little boy would become the next Roger Milla who attracted the admiration of the world by singlehandedly thrashing Columbia, Romania and almost wiped the smiles off British fans' faces in Italy. But the Three Lions, the English National Team, had a lucky escape and won over The Indomitable Lions of Cameroon at the quarter final stage.

My father wanted me to play football so badly that he bought me a set of brand new uniforms and playing shoes. I ran all the way to the playing ground of the school not far from our house every weekend. But I was never picked for the team. My Dad found out that I wasn't playing and came up with the genius idea of bribing the coach. As a result, I was picked one day to play the last few minutes of a game. I was terrible. I was so bad that I caused an own-goal, costing my team an outright victory.

The second time I was entrusted with the striker's position, I still didn't know what I was doing when I found myself in front of my goalkeeper. I caused a penalty and once more, we lost the game. I was dropped and sent home the same day by the coach who asked me not to come back. I was a bit relieved because I was not interested in football. My Dad was my only fan.

Daddy genuinely wanted the best for us and went to great lengths to make sure of that. When we were in primary school, he got acquainted with our teachers. He got to know them, found out where they lived and usually invited them to local bars. He got them some drinks and money only so that myself and my brother would have special attention in class. This was really an issue for us sometimes but it paid off because we never had to go through the same class twice until we graduated. We were well-dressed with brand new uniforms at the beginning of each school year. We also had enough pocket allowance unlike some of our school mates whose families were worse off.

At home, there was an apparent harmony. But over a relatively short period of time, animosity gained grounds between my parents.

Mummy had a very nice singing voice that made her very popular among her peers. Her efforts to become a superstar in the community overshadowed her home duties as a mother and as a wife.

Her increasing addiction to the attention she was getting from the outside made her lose control on the inside. She became very distant and always absent in the home. She would go out in mid-afternoon only to return late at night, usually drunk. Daddy was gradually running out of patience.

I was only about twelve or thirteen and could witness the growing rift in the family because of my mother's intolerable behaviour. I also foresaw the long term damage on my father's reputation as a proud man and the impact on us as a family. I tried as best as I could to warn my mother that her loud voice and bad temper was affecting my studies and school results. In response to my protest, she would hit me right in the face.

There were times when I went to school with swollen eyes for crying for hours the night before. The perfect family in which I was growing up was falling apart. I knew that a day would come when Daddy would get sick and tired of it all and as a consequence, would turn into a very different person. Although I was too young at the time to make such a dire prediction, the years that followed proved me right. My father had become unrecognisable.

In 1994, I decided to get stronger to defend myself against the bullies. But to be more accurate, I really needed self-confidence. I had been pushed around too much and was getting sick of it. I started doing a number of physically challenging sports. One of those was kickboxing. I got hurt quite a lot in the training process but I kept coming back for more. I felt that I was doing something right for myself. The pain gave me more motivation, more determination. It was as if getting hurt was preparing me for something greater in the future. I trained hard and built some lean muscles to impress my first crush at school.

Eveline was her name and she was the same age as me. Her skin was a lot darker than mine and her hair was short like that of a boy. She stuttered a little bit and I found that cute. Unfortunately, she did not like me as much as I liked her. But because I was trying to find new ways to win her over, I learned to do backflips. I had seen her once clapping for another boy who had done two in the school yard during the mid-morning break. At one point, I could do up to five or six in a row. But even that did not help me to win her attention.

The other thing that I could do was the splits on two chairs like Jean Claude Van Damme in his movies. My goal was to become as big and as strong as Jean Claude Van Damme, Arnold Schwarzenegger in *Terminator* and Dolph Lundgren in *Universal Soldier*. I actually manifested meeting these people in real life in London during my adult years - more on that in Chapter Ten.

A year later, my performance at school was beginning to weaken as a consequence of my commitment to my training. I decided to cut down on sports and to focus on my studies. I also wanted to earn some extra money. I needed spare cash for trips to the Cinema and also to, occasionally, help my poorer friends. I wanted to buy a new radio set for my newly allocated bedroom in the family home.

I saved enough cash over a period of a few months and got myself a second hand Nokia camera. It was really bad and produced poor quality pictures, but I was a good guy at school and charged half the normal price for taking pictures of students in class or standing by a flower bucket. I then set enough money aside to get a better camera with which I made the amount I needed to buy all the little things I wanted. However, the radio was too expensive. I went to Daddy and explained that I was a bit short. He was so proud of me that he actually gave me a little more than what I needed and I purchased a better radio set for my bedroom. I was fifteen.

In 1996, my Dad had his break in the business world. He had a few white friends who brought him some books from Europe about the natural resources, the fauna and flora of Africa in general but of Cameroon in particular. As ready as he was, an opportunity came his way that later made him a lot of money, a fortune compared to what he was making working for the government.

One of his friends, a French man, came back from France after a short holiday and made him the suggestion to start exporting live aquatic fishes for aquariums in Europe. The French man provided my Dad with some packaging material and training manuals in the livestock export sector. Before long, I was working with my Dad collecting various species of fish from different parts of the country and exporting them to France.

A few months later, the business grew and our stock list expanded to aquatic plants, live reptiles, invertebrates and amphibians. The destinations expanded to many more countries in Europe, Asia and the USA. Money started to come in increasing amounts through multiple sources on a continuous basis.

Daddy was not illiterate, but he could not speak or read English. That was my job at the tender age of sixteen. I would read, translate and reply to clients around the world on behalf of my father. In the process, I was learning and improving, becoming the best student in my class in languages in general, but particularly in English.

In 1997, a fax arrived from Das Tropen Paradies, a German reptile wholesale company, that had just started in the business and had heard of us in the German magazine that we had advertised in. The company belonged to two of the nicest people I have ever known: Volker Ennenbach and Thorsten Holtman. I had just chosen German as my third language in high school and loved it. I saw the opportunity to improve my German vocabulary.

I was fascinated by that language; it conveyed strength and authority. I wanted to impress these new clients and the best way I could think of, was to write to them in German in response to their fax written in English. I used my old and crumbling German/French dictionary to find the most impressive words. I wanted to come across as knowledgable as possible to our new partners.

I introduced myself to them as my Dad's partner and implied that I had shares in the company. Of course the reality was different. We successfully shipped invertebrates, reptiles and amphibians to them and they liked the service, the follow up and the flow of communication between their company and ours.

It was time to move up a notch in my mission to impress even more.

I wanted to speak to them over the phone as I had been communicating only via faxes up to that point. I spent time practicing, reading and listening to German tapes. My German teacher at school liked the efforts I was putting into my homework and helped me with some of the tapes that he had brought back from his teacher training in Germany a year earlier.

Thorsten Holtman was twenty-seven and I was seventeen when we started trading together and we got on very well from the outset. We spoke on the phone in German for the first time and I knew that I had found someone that was going to have a significant impact on my life. Our phone conversations usually took a couple of days to set up.

I would give him a time and the number of a public phone booth. Then, I would go there to wait for his call. Amongst other things, we discussed shipments and payments. He once asked me how I could be so fluent in such a difficult language. My answer was that I simply loved it enough to put in the effort required to learn it. This exchange between us lasted for a few months during my school term. Although I did not tell my german friend during our numerous phone conversations, I was aiming for something that was more important to me than anything else in the world.

# CHAPTER TWO

# The Other Side

---

The business was doing very well. Daddy was happy and I was excited to be part of that adventure. Money was owing in various amounts and at regular intervals. But my parents became increasingly distant and the home atmosphere got heavier by the day.

I was not getting paid for my services and it didn't bother me because after all, we had plenty of good quality food to eat and a roof over our heads. Unlike most family homes around, ours had a colour television set, a fridge and our floor was cemented. I was proud to be contributing to the business and helping my father take care of our family. I didn't have a say in how the money we made together was spent. Daddy was spending what he called HIS money on anything and everything that he wanted without consulting anyone. I did not expect him to involve me in the household expenditure.

After all, I was a minor living at home. What I thought was wrong of him was that he did not involve his wife, my mother, who was systematically excluded from decisions regarding money. Sometimes, she was not even consulted about what we should eat for dinner. Although she was the one doing the cooking, Daddy went as far as doing the groceries shopping himself. I found that very strange and distressing.

Mummy, like me, was noticing changes in Daddy's behaviour. She was also gradually realising that she had gotten too far in her quest for celebrity status amongst her friends. As a consequence, her husband had run out of patience and started to care less and less about her and what she was doing. His attitude changed further as payments from clients grew even larger. The kind and caring family man that we all loved gradually turned into a cold, insensitive and emotionless human being.

My siblings were too young to understand what was going on. Being the first- born, I found it increasingly hard to watch my parents argue all the time. Their quarrels started with simple disagreements every now and then to full blown nasty accusations of infidelity. Their egos had grown out of proportion and my childhood home was their battlefield. I felt so affected that I wished I could disappear into thin air.

I met three girls at school whom I became very close to. They gave me the emotional support without which I would have simply lost my mind. I believe that their friendship was really a Godsend. They were: Murielle, Josephine and Germaine. We all met in high school and became inseparable. They knew everything that was happening in my family and I knew everything about theirs. In actual fact, what was going on in those girls' families made me realise that despite everything, I was a lucky boy.

Murielle was abandoned by her father at the age of eight and was living with her mother and a step-father who was not the protective father figure she hoped for. She later got married prematurely at the age of twenty to an abusive man with whom she had two children. Her marriage lasted eight years. She is currently, in the year 2022, single and still grappling with life's challenges.

Germaine lived with her mother who died in a road accident just when I was writing this book. Her father left the family home when she was a teenager and moved in with a younger woman. He spent twenty five years in a neighbouring country before returning home with a sickness that eventually took his life in 2015. Germaine now lives with her husband and three children.

Josephine came from a polygamous family of sixteen children in which parental attention was in short supply. She is a proud mother of four and is still unmarried at the moment of writing this book.

With that in mind and in comparison, I really had the best family environment. I had both parents and all of my siblings living together under the same roof. The business was doing well and my family gained respect from neighbours and relatives. Everything looked perfect on the outside but things were rotten on the inside.

My father accused me of being my mother's accomplice in her adultery escapades. He condemned me so unforgivingly because I refused to turn against her in his favour. He tried numerous times to give me a very bleak image of my mother. But I kept saying that I only had one mother and one father and believed that neither was replaceable. Daddy did not consider a neutral position; which I was actually doing my best to accommodate.

As a teenage boy, it was extremely hard to watch my mother constantly in tears. I saw her get more wrinkled and lose a significant amount of weight in only a few weeks. All I kept thinking was my multiple warnings to her a few years prior. If she had listened to me, I truly believe that most of her sadness could have been avoided. But because she did not, I was now caught up in the middle of a constant marital feud.

We discovered later that my father was the one playing away. He had a little girl below the age of five in another city and was paying for expensive holidays for his mistress and their child to France a couple of times a year. He even had pictures of his other family lying around in the bedroom in our home. We found them one day during a routine clean up.

That was the first time I lost the admiration I had for my father. Although he caused a lot of emotional pain to my mother with his words, I still believed that he would do the right thing in due course and needed a bit of time. But when we found out about his other family, I was very disappointed and wanted to leave home. It was just too much. But leaving was not an option; I was too involved in the business to drop everything at once. I had all of our business partners to remain in contact with and school to think of.

A few weeks later, around April of 1997, my new German friend, Thorsten sent a fax addressed to me that changed everything. It was written in German and translated as follows:

*"Dear Charly, find below the list of livestock that we would like in our next shipment. We are getting ready to attend Europe's biggest reptiles show in Hamm [That is in the north of Germany] and we would like you to come with the next shipment. We will take care of all the expenses and you will be returning to Cameroon with the payment of the shipment in cash."*

Oh Wow!

That was exactly what I hoped for. I was being invited to visit Germany, meet my new friends and get to know their families. But more importantly, I would get to practice and improve my eloquence in German. That was simply the best thing that could have happened to me at that time. I explained what the fax said to my father and he was happy. Very happy because that shipment was the biggest we had made up to that point to the Germans and as a result, the payment was going to be substantial. Also, the proud and egotistical man that he was realised that he had a great opportunity to brag about his success in the community. He was sending his son to Europe and all of his friends, the neighbours and anybody who would listen or not, heard about it.

The weeks that followed my invitation were exciting. There was a sudden feeling of peace at home. I was sure nothing had really changed, but I was no longer affected by the negativity and drama of my environment. I had a very different interpretation of the events around me and the fact that I had something meaningful to look forward to gave me a different kind of energy and vitality.

I realised that the main cause of my sorrow was not what was happening at home. It was, as I look back now, the lack of something to look forward to. Nothing had changed at home but with such an exciting event not too far in the future, my mind was buzzing so much that I no longer paid attention to my reality.

My mother was happy for me, but knew that my trip to Europe was going to make my father even more unbearable. I cared about her welfare but going to Germany was a great opportunity and I could not let anything take that chance away from me. I told no-one at school except my three best friends, Murielle, Germaine and Josephine.

In the first week of June 1997, Thorsten sent me the invitation I needed for my visa application along with a contact name at the German embassy in Yaoundé, the capital of Cameroon. I followed the instructions I was given and a three months, single entry visa, was issued to me with no complications. I knew it was summer time in Europe between June and August and got ready for my trip accordingly. I spent all of the cash I had saved up to that point from my school photography to buy some African fancy clothes and traditional shoes as gifts for my hosts and their families. My Dad also bought some handicraft and decorations for the people who would be my family for the following eight weeks.

The shipment I was travelling with got put together. The reptiles came from all corners of the country, packed according to the client's instructions and boxed up in accordance with the International Air Transport Association (IATA). Then came the time to have the experience of my life.

On Saturday 28 of June 1997, it was the flight Sabena [former Brussels Airlines] that took me from Douala to Frankfurt via Brussels and take-off time was 23:40 local time. The reptiles' boxes had to be taken care of first. Daddy and I went to the Cargo area of the airport to deal with the shipment's formalities. After everything was done, I became the centre of attention.

No-one in my family had ever been on an aeroplane. I was the first. A very proud moment for me but also for everyone. As we got to the departure lounge, we were joined by Parfait and Jackson, two of my siblings and four other excited cousins.

My mother did not come to the airport as I expected.

I felt her absence at this special moment and that feeling was more than just her not being there physically. The feeling was much deeper than that; it was the fact that I could not see her pride for me in her eyes. I hoped that she would come to wish me a safe journey to an unknown land. My father was in a very good mood on that day at the airport. I thought about asking where my mother was and then, I changed my mind. I realised that any question about her would have spoiled the joyous atmosphere.

She had decided to stay home with the younger children. But I know she could have made the necessary arrangements to be there if she had wanted to. The truth is that she did not want to be next to him, the man she once said yes to, but was now frightened of.

I had a little farewell conversation with those present. Everybody had an idea of what I should do when I got to Germany. My father wanted me to make loads of friends and new connections for more business possibilities in the future. My brothers suggested that I do not return home. According to them, it would be better if I stayed in Germany, worked hard and sent loads of money to our mother who was, at that point, almost destitute despite living with a man with a bulky bank account.

My cousins just wanted gifts from Europe, nothing specific, just anything that I could get my hands on.

It was time to go, the plane was due to leave in less than an hour. The passport checking and travel formalities were done quite swiftly. I headed down the cold corridor as my senses enjoyed the aromatic smell of the cold air inside. The groaning of the plane's engines grew louder as I approached the entry of the plane. I was welcomed by a very pretty svelte woman with long dark hair with a bright smile. With the palm of her left hand, she pointed in the direction of my seat after checking my boarding pass. I felt like I was floating and gliding between the seats, going pass people fumbling with their seat belts and overhead bags.

I took my seat and admired the beauty of my surroundings. I could not believe that I was finally in the engine that I saw for the first time and fell in love with at five years old . I could see that not everyone on the plane was going to the same destination. It felt like the United Nations with different languages, nationalities and races represented.

The pilot introduced himself and assured us that the journey would be smooth with no disturbance to Brussels where the landing was scheduled at 06:20 am local time after six hours flight. During the summer months, there is an hour difference between Europe and Central Africa where I was flying from. So, it would be 05:20 am at home when we land in the Belgian capital.

The plane pulled off the terminal and slowly moved towards the runway and stopped suddenly. The captain, with a soft Flemish accent, informed us that there was a plane ahead of us and that we would be moving shortly after. During that short stand-still, a picture flashed into my awareness. It was that of my mother. I wondered what Daddy was going to say to her that night. He had a way with language and knew how to hit her in her core and cause a flood of tears with his carelessly chosen words.

The emotional abuse he was inflicting on her was unbearable. I had a feeling, during that short standstill, that with me gone and my siblings too young, he was going to be even more unkind. Though he never raised his hand at her, she was at the mercy of his sharp tongue. It was incredible to find out how much help and comfort could be given to a person by practicing what the Vietnamese Buddhist Thich Nhat Hanh calls "deep listening" in his amazing book *True Love*.

Deep listening, according to the buddhists, is a step beyond being quiet while the other person speaks. It is bringing the self fully in the present moment and not only pay an undivided attention to the words, but also, connect with the emotions of the person speaking. That is something that I mastered as a teenager in the process of comforting my mother when she needed someone to talk to.

Her own siblings were never there for her. On the contrary, they resented her for various reasons. Although things weren't going well in her marriage, my mother still had a husband and was not suffering the physical violence that her sisters had gone through, from men who abused them. One of my unmarried Aunties, on my mother's side, had three children from two failed relationships and was openly envious of what my mother seemed to have going on in her home. But her envy was based, solely, on appearances.

I suddenly came back to myself in the soft leather covered seat on that plane as it pushed forward and began a speedy glide on the runway to take off. As it climbed steeply in the atmosphere, I had a sick feeling in my churning stomach. After a few seconds, everything came back to normal. The plane steadied itself and took a full horizontal position in the air and for the first time - I was flying.

It seemed that the early part of the flight was not everybody's favourite, judging by the look of discomfort on some passengers' faces. I sat by the window and the people next to me, a couple, didn't stop giggling and chatting in French. They were describing the fun they had in the forest of the southern part of Cameroon and the beautiful people that they met. Hearing those comments brought some joy to my heart. It was nice to hear positive things being said about my country.

But that reputation was short-lived. Cameroon won the top spot of the most corrupt countries in the world for two years in a row - 1998 and 1999 before losing it to neighbouring Nigeria in the year 2000.

On that plane, all I wanted was to enjoy the sounds, the smells and the sights. Nothing else was more important. About an hour into the flight, we were handed the onboard menus, duvet covers and headsets. A little after that, we were served dinner and then it was time to have some sleep. But I could not shut my eyes. The adrenaline would not allow me to and if I had tried, my worries about my mother would keep me awake. I decided to go for some distractions. I watched the movies offered onboard until we landed in Brussels.

After a quick forty- five minutes transit, I was on a connecting flight to Frankfurt - Germany. The plane landed and I got off. Although I had no sleep during the flight, I felt energised. I was allowed through the immigration control after an unchallenging process. I collected my two bags, placed them on one of the available trolleys and headed towards the exit. It suddenly occurred to me that I didn't know what my hosts looked like.

I knew they were white Germans, but I was at a German airport full of white people and I was not sure what to do next. I thought about screaming a name out. But I was not sure which name to call; Volker or Thorsten? Or just wait somewhere and expect a tap on my shoulder. Really silly thoughts but I didn't know better. This was my first experience. My friends had it all figured out.

As I walked down the exit corridor, I saw a medium-height man with what looked like medical glasses. He wore a plain blue t-shirt, a pair of short-cut blue jeans and black shoes. It was Thorsten. He held an A4 white paper with, Charly Ngouh, clearly handwritten on it. I headed towards him. He looked at me straight in the face, gave me a chirpy smile and a warm embrace. He then said : *"Herzlich* Willkommen im Deutschland mein Freund" - Welcome to Germany my friend.

On that Sunday 29th of June 1997, at around 10:30 am local time, Thorsten helped me with the bags and we exited the airport together. We got to the blue minivan he had come with and he invited me to take a seat in the front after loading the bags in the rear. We started our four hours journey from Frankfurt to Oberhausen. The scenery was magnificent: huge buildings, clean roads, organised traffic, unambiguous direction signs and perfectly synchronised traffic lights. Some fresh air was blowing through the half opened windows and I was truly in a state of fascination.

Thorsten spoke to me in German. Although I was a bit slow and frequently asked him to repeat and to speak more distinctly, I would eventually understand. He offered to speak in English, but I refused because I was eager to get into the discomfort that comes from learning something different or improving something familiar.

I wanted to make the most of the opportunity I had to work on my German and luckily, my new friend accommodated my request and the conversation continued. He asked me about my family, my dreams, my long-term goals. The answers I gave him were vague and unspecific. At that point, I could not quite see myself without my father and his business. I could not make it alone. After all, at the age of seventeen, I was legally a minor.

We got to his house at around 14:00 and his wife, Kirstin, had prepared some freshly baked bread, a few tasty looking German sausages, some salad and yogurt. After I had exchanged some civilities with Mrs. Holtman, I was invited to help myself to the food available. But before that I needed to take a shower.

I went to the small but comfortable room that was prepared for me to get changed. The walls of the inside were painted in grey. It had a night stand, a small flower bucket, a television set, a wardrobe and a shoe-rack. The mattress on the single bed was fitted with strings.

The duvet cover was bright white with red petals spread all over it and one word printed in capital letters: *"Willkommen!"* - Welcome! .

When I stepped into the bathroom, I did not realise that the small plastic bottle in the corner of the bathtub contained a shower gel. I had never used or seen one before. I grabbed the hand wash soap that was placed on the sink and used it to shower with. After the shower, I dried myself using the towel that was placed on my bed. Then I poured the shower gel in my hand and rubbed it all over my body thinking that it was a moisturising lotion. As I wasn't sure about the smell, I wrapped the towel around my waist and went to ask Kirstin in the kitchen across the small corridor. She told me that it was a shower gel. I had to shower again.

I ate very little that first day and because I had been awake for over thirty-six hours, I started to feel drained. I went to bed for some much needed sleep. I was meeting Volker the next day at the office. The reptiles' cargo I had brought with me was going to be delivered by a freight carrier the following morning after custom clearance.

The next day, I got up early, feeling very happy with a great deal of anticipation to what was going to happen during my first full day in Germany. Kirstin made me an omelette that I ate with some freshly baked bread from the local bakery across the street. I washed everything down with a glass of sweet apple juice. Thorsten had a cup of coffee, then read the morning paper that was delivered to the front door. At around eight O'clock, we left the house after he had given a kiss to his wife and said *"Ich liebe dich!"* - I love you!

I had never witnessed such a loving and tender relationship between two adults. Although my parents loved us and cared for us when my siblings and I were little, we never saw them express that kind of love to each other. I was more accustomed to them having arguments and acting like strangers at war. Kirstin repeated the same words back to her loving man before wishing us both a good day. We left and drove to the office where I met Volker. He looked strange to me with his ponytail and funny beard. His voice sounded a little feminine and his accent was a lot heavier than Thorsten's; which made him a lot more difficult to understand at first. He was very nice and fatherly to me at the age of only thirty six. He called me: *"Charly mein Sohn"* - Charly my son.

The reptiles' boxes got unpacked and fifteen percent of the animals were dead on arrival. That meant I would be returning home with eighty five percent of the total invoice; which was in the region of five or six thousand USD Dollars. A tremendous amount of money for a business that was only a few months old.

I called my father and that information was all he wanted to know. He never even asked me how my journey was, if I was warmly welcomed or where I was staying. Absolutely nothing about my journey. His only interest was to know how much money I will be bringing home. I gave him the amount and before our conversation ended, he reminded me to make new contacts and to advertise our livestock to everybody I met.

A few days later, when I managed to speak to my mother and she told me that everything was ne at home. But I could feel that it wasn't the case. I did not insist and took her words at face value. I asked her about Edmond, the sixth child in our family. She reassured me that he was doing great. He was five years old and could not speak or walk as a result of the meningitis he caught a few months after his birth. He suffered a number of health complications but fortunately, he recovered well and is now a very healthy man.

For the following eight weeks, I improved my German through daily practice. I also got a better understanding of our trade and the care of reptiles in captivity. My awareness expanded and I started to see things differently. I evaluated the potential of our market and did not feel the need to stay in Germany. One of Thorsten 's friend offered to adopt me. I was a minor and he was willing to welcome me into his home for an unlimited period of time. But I decided to return and help Daddy expand the family business.

I returned home in late August 1997 with an avalanche of ideas and techniques to improve our activities. But I did not anticipate my father's reaction. He was reluctant to invest money in the improvement of the care of animals before shipping. That, in my opinion, would have enhanced the quality of our livestock, lowered our DOA (Dead On Arrival) rate and increased our RIO (Return On Investment). He opted for cheap, easy and quick fixes to do business despite having enough money to be professional. He saw me as a child and did not share my vision. That was very frustrating to me and I became unhappy. I was still at school and things had not improved at home between my parents.

Sometimes, Daddy would disappear for days and we would not know where he was. When he returned, he generally spoke to no- one. Not even to me other than to check whether a client had settled an invoice. If it wasn't the case, he would willingly work with me to chase late payments. Once the money arrived, he would go quiet again.

I wanted to escape. I walked for two hours every time I felt sad to get to the Douala International Airport (DLA) where, in some magical ways, I found peace. I reminded myself of that initial visit when I was five years old and suddenly, my sense of joy returned. The people, the smells, the eagerness of people leaving and the excitement of those arriving made me forget my situation, though for a little while. There were times when I left the house for two or three days and slept on benches just to get Daddy's attention. But he did not notice that I was screaming on the inside, longing for the father I once admired. I never stayed away for too long. I knew that any extended absence would adversely affect my mother and my siblings who looked up to me.

I wondered why my Dad behaved in that way for a very long time in my adult years. I always knew, looking back at my earlier years, that he was genuinely a good man. However, it occurred to me that he did not select his friends wisely. He was successful in business, but all of his friends were down and out. They were a bunch of drunks who cheated on their wives, had children in numerous parts of the city and lacked ambition.

My Dad was doing well in life and business but fell short of creating an environment that was conducive to his progress. His friends were heading south while he was heading north and the gravitational pull of mediocrity from those people was too strong. Although more money kept coming in, life did not really get better in terms of peace of mind and contentment. My father wanted to do good, but his environment was stronger than his will.

That is a very important fact to acknowledge at this stage in the story. That information sets me, the writer of this book, and the reader on a different path than the one my father chose. He might have decided to stay with his old friends in his new life either by ignorance or by arrogance to show off his opulence. But we now have a better understating of the effect of the environment that we choose for ourselves.

In 1998, on my eighteenth birthday, my Dad gave me money to throw a party by the beach to celebrate my adulthood. But I had a feeling that I was already an adult long before then considering all the things I dealt with. That year went  quickly and I did not get an invitation to travel to Germany; it came the following year.

In 1999, I returned to Germany after another invitation from my friends. This time I knew where everything was and what everybody did at the shop.

Because I was a little older, my German friends asked me to work for them to earn some money. I got to handle new species of reptiles up close. But my main duties revolved around washing and cleaning the cages where the livestock was exposed. I was paid Two Deutsch Mark per cage. The job was tiring but, nonetheless, rewarding.

One evening, during a business dinner, I met Martin Davey, a businessman from New Zealand. He was well known in the animal export industry and mainly specialised in large mammals and birds of prey. I was sat across the table from him while we were eating. He was very impressed with my knowledge of the reptile trade and even more so by the fact that I could speak German and English besides French. He gave me his business card and our conversation opened another chapter in my life.

Before leaving Germany to return to Cameroon, I was informed by a friend that I had failed my high school exam. As a result of that, I was not able to proceed to University. Although I was very disappointed, I realised that my heart was no longer in furthering my education in a conventional setting. I had learned a lot from my visits in Germany and from the exchanges I had with experienced people in the live animal trade.

When I got back from Europe that second time, I decided to focus on business. I was only nineteen but I knew what I wanted. I decided to leave school to find my own way. I e-mailed Martin in Prague, Czech republic, where he had an office and we communicated over a few months. That same year, my father almost did something that would have changed the dynamics and the make up of our family.

Since he no longer considered that my mother was worthy of his time and attention, he decided to get a second wife. With the support of his own mother, my grand mother, he began the process of marrying a university graduate who was only three years older than me.

My grandmother was very protective of my father and his siblings. She had raised them by herself. But what I found rather strange in this situation was, she was pushing my Dad to do to my mother what was done to her. She was the wife of a man who, after fifteen years of marriage, threw her out of the home and got himself a younger woman.

Polygamy was, and still is, allowed in my country. But the bride and the groom have to agree on the type of marriage they are entering into. If it is polygamy, the bride would be consenting to the groom marrying one or more women during their time together. That is an arrangement that was common when my parents got together but quite rare nowadays.

Mummy and Daddy had signed  for a monogamy partnership in marriage; which essentially meant that the bride would be the groom's only wife for as long as they remained married. Something that my grandmother did not comprehend as she argued for a second wife; a legally unacceptable undertaking.

My father knew that an extra marital union was not legally bound. The only way he could have a new wife in accordance to the law was to divorce my mother. But with six children and most of them in their teenage years, it was not an easy decision to make. My mother remained serene and did nothing to stop father's lustful ambition. In the end, the second marriage did not happen. We never found out why the young educated woman changed her mind. She most probably foresaw the complexity of my father's situation after her only visit into our home.

Martin sent me an invitation to visit the Czech Republic for a few months and his staff to train me. He already had three companies working in synergy from Texas in the USA, Christ Church in New Zealand and Prague. I was going to become the director of his fourth company with the sole objective of running projects in Sub-Saharan Africa.

In the year 2000, at twenty years old, events were moving fast in my life. Daddy gradually loosened his grip on me. I was ambitious beyond my years and he understood that it was time to allow me to clear my own path. He encouraged me to go to Czech Republic for further training. My success was also the success of the family, he said.

There was a problem however. I needed a Czech visa and there wasn't a Czech diplomatic representation in

Cameroon. The only way to get a visa was to travel to a neighbouring country to submit a visa application. Nigeria turned out to be the best option.

I travelled to Lagos, initially for two days to get my visa application processed. But right after I had landed in that populous Nigerian city, a fuel strike caused an unrest that lasted four days. I witnessed horror during that time. Vehicles were burned in every corner, people chased around and brutalised by the police and gun shots in all directions every couple of minutes. The place was in total disarray. I locked myself in my hotel bedroom and watched the events unfold on television and through my glass window. Despite all of this, I found my way to the Czech embassy where my visa application was rejected at first. Then, after a quick review and some guarantees from Martin, the visa was granted.

I was in possession of a thirty day Czech tourist visa. Someone at the hotel tried to snatch it from me. One evening, a tall dark and chubby man came to my room and pretended to be a policeman. He asked me to show him my papers and I almost gave him everything. Suddenly, it occurred to me that he did not show me his police Identification. I asked for it politely and he became uneasy. He raised his voice and I screamed. When other guests came to my room to find out what was happening, the fake policeman turned round and said that he was just kidding.

I returned to Cameroon and five days later, I was on a Swiss aeroplane bound for Prague via Zurich. On the day of my trip, I turned up at the airport with a poisonous snake. A viper that I was carrying in a sealed bucket as hand luggage. At the checking desk, when I said what the small red container had inside, everyone panicked. I almost got thrown off the flight. Luckily, my surname sounded familiar to the airport security forces who knew my father. The unwanted reptile was taken away and I was allowed to fly.

I arrived in Prague during the summer of the year 2000. Martin picked me up from the airport and when we arrived at his office, he introduced me to his staff. I was warmly welcomed by everybody and allocated a room to stay in, just above the office. Martin shared his bedroom with Dana, his partner in life and in business. He was estranged from his wife who still lived in New Zealand with his two grown up children.

My visa needed to be extended so that I could stay longer in Prague. But by law, such an extension could not be granted in the country and I had to travel to Poland for my visa extension. The accounting staff at the office gave me a return ticket to the neighbouring country along with all the necessary documents for my application. I went to Warsaw for four days and during that time I met the most beautiful girl I had ever seen. She had short coloured hair and her name was Silvia. I met her at a bus stop on my way to the Warsaw zoo. I was trying to find out which bus to get onto when she noticed that I was struggling with directions on the map. She tapped me gently on the right shoulder and asked me If she could help.

Her English was good, but she was better. She told me which bus to get on and I convinced her to come with me. She agreed after hesitating and deliberating for a few minutes. We spent that day together at the zoo and it felt amazing. She told me that she was eighteen years old and was born in a small village in the North of Poland. She was in the capital city to study biology.

My stay in Poland went rather fast and after I had submitted my application at the Czech embassy, I had to leave.

On the day of my departure, my heart sank when I left Silvia standing on the platform alone as my train glided away. We had only spent three days together and had so much fun that I did not realise how fast time had flown by. She had a little puppy dog that I was beginning to get attached to. I looked at her through the windows of the train and she was in tears. The separation was hard on the two of us. We remained in touch for a few months after that until I sadly lost her number. Unfortunately, social media hadn't been created yet and losing her details bugged me for years. I never saw her again and later assumed that certain things in life were not meant to be. I had to move on.

I got back to Prague with a temporary visa valid for six months, the processing period for my residency. I worked for a few more weeks with Martin, Dana, and their employees before returning to Cameroon to apply everything that I was taught about the export of mammals and large wild birds.

Unfortunately, rampant corruption and red tape made my efforts fruitless. Every attempt I made to be professional and productive were impeded by corrupt and greedy officials. Martin grew impatient and pulled the plug on the whole project. But before he did that, one shipment of small monkeys to the London Zoo was a success. He travelled to Cameroon to make sure himself that everything was done properly. It was our first shipment together. It was also an opportunity for him to meet my family. He gave me 2000 US dollars in cash as payment for the monkeys' shipment because I was the person he dealt with all along. I later handed every penny of that lump sum to my father who had done nothing on that project. I had taken care of everything and all I got was 50 dollars for a job well done. Martin left Cameroon and things never really picked up after that.

A few weeks later, I received an e-mail from the Czech embassy in Warsaw informing me that my residency application was successful. I sent my passport to Poland by DHL and after it had been endorsed with a two years multiple entry visa to the Czech Republic, it was returned to me by normal post. I never received it. To date, I don't know which direction my passport took when it got to Cameroon. But I suspect that it was stolen by the post office staff. That was the end of my Czech fairy tale.

In 2001 and at the age of twenty-one , I was lost and not sure what to do next. My travel documents were stolen and I couldn't go to university because I had failed my exam the year before. Moreover, I really didn't want to be at home watching the never-ending parental conflicts. My options were very limited, but there was one thing I could still do: I re-sat my exams. I pulled out my old school notes and studied like my life depended on it for three months. In the end my determination paid off. I passed my high school exam with honours. Even my Dad who told me that it was a waste of time was speechless when he saw the results.

I could now apply to study in the USA. But something happened that dashed my hopes of studying in the United Sates - The attacks on the World Trade Centre in New York on Sep 11, 2001.

I had to submit my application for the course as soon as possible because money was available and I knew that unless I acted quickly, my Dad could change his mind. After the attacks in America, my father and I decided to look elsewhere and the next best choice was - The United Kingdom.

# CHAPTER THREE

# The Cold Feeling

---

I looked into various possibilities to study in the United Kingdom and my relentless search led me to The New School of English in Cambridge. It was the perfect language school for me. I read the positive reviews online by former students from countries around the world and instantly knew that I had to stop searching. The school was located only a few minutes walk away from the Cambridge city centre and close to the train station with regular connections to London.

The English spoken in the United Kingdom was somewhat different. I had listened to tapes from the local British council and some broadcasts on the BBC radio. I realised that I would struggle if I didn't start with lessons immediately upon arriving. But I also did not want to wait until I arrived in Cambridge to work on my English. I decided to only read materials written in English and stayed away from those in French during that time.

I communicated with the admin office of the school and after a few emails, I received the necessary forms; which I completed and returned by fax. My father agreed to transfer a small deposit to the provided account and I was accepted on a six months intensive English course.

The package that I chose had a provision for accommodation in a host family. I was also entitled to breakfast and dinner every day for the duration of my course. It was a very expensive offer from the school, but money was no issue at that time and I did not worry about the high cost of my course. Daddy had consented to cover all the expenses related to my studies in the United Kingdom.

I received all the registration papers and other documents from the school a couple of weeks later. Along with some financial information and bank slips from my father who also was my sponsor, I submitted a student visa application to the British High Commission in Cameroon. After my application was received, I was told that the process would take eight weeks. I was given an appointment card to report to a special envoy sent from London to conduct long term visa interviews on Wednesday 14 of November 2001 at 11.00 am.

The two months between my application and the interview date were the longest of my life. I could not think of anything else. I really had no alternative, no Plan B. I was really all in and going to England was, as I saw it, my escape from a life of constant pain. I thought of my previous failures and strongly believed that they were all leading to a better life for me away from a home that I no longer felt part of.

My two younger brothers stepped in to help our father in different roles. I personally detached myself from all the business activities and became a sort of adviser. My brothers came to me on a regular basis to complain about Daddy's thoughtless decisions and lack of clear business strategy. I simply asked them to be patient and accommodating to a man who was reluctant to change.

I spent all my days thinking of all the wonderful things I was going to do in England, the people I would meet at my school and the possibilities that would become available to me. I continuously listened to the BBC radio station to familiarise myself with the new world that I was about to enter and rejected any form of distraction. I did not, at any moment, think of the possibility of not being granted a student visa. It was like I already had it and was waiting for a departure date.

I also made sure that I remained in good terms with my sponsor who, I knew could have stopped the process at any time if I had said or done anything that he did not approve of. I even asked my mother to do her best to avoid needless arguments and to help improve the atmosphere at home. I needed Daddy to be in a constant good mood. No-one really benefited from all the drama anyway!

The big day finally came and I reported to the British High Commission for my interview. The events of that day will remain with me for as long as I live.

I had travelled the day before from Douala, where I lived, to Yaoundé, the capital city of my country and checked into a very cheap hotel for one night. My alarm clock went off at 06:00 am on that Wednesday 14th of November 2001 and I got up with a headache caused by the lack of proper sleep. The night had been long and every possibility crossed my mind. I was worried but excited at the same time.

I arrived at the High Commission with hours to spare. I planned to spend the time I had before my interview to practice the questions that I thought the interviewer would ask. I had written them on a piece of paper that I kept in my pocket. Those questions were the result of an investigation that I had carried out by reaching out to people who had failed the same interview that I was about to attend.

My investigation was wide and not limited to interviews for British visas. I also gathered questions from people whose applications were rejected by different European embassies. I had about twenty questions and I went through them all trying to come up with the best and most convincing answers. The most delicate question on my list was the following:

"will you come back to Cameroon after your studies? If yes, why?"

The best answer I had was:

"Yes - I will return to Cameroon after my studies because my father is running a successful business and as his first child , I will take over from him after enhancing my skills and knowledge through my studies in the United Kingdom.", not too bad, I thought.

The time for the interview came and myself with the other applicants were invited to wait in the foyer adjacent to the interview room. There were eight of us waiting for our fifteen- minutes slots.

I appeared to be the youngest candidate in the waiting room. We were all nervous and some of us could hardly breathe normally. It was my fourth visa interview to travel to Europe. I had attended two to visit Germany and one to travel to Czech Republic and knowing that I had a successful track record, I remained calm. The three men sitting opposite me were sweating even though, the waiting room was fully air-conditioned. The guy to my left was rubbing his hands between his thighs and the lady to my right had her arms crossed.

At some point, I smiled and asked that lady what she was going to England for. She replied that it was for medical reasons. Her daughter was married to an Englishman and they lived in Manchester, in the north of England, with their two children. She told me that she had visited the UK a few times before and showed me her previous visas in her worn out passport. I had travelled before too but I could not prove it. All of my previous passports were stolen and attending that interview was a new beginning for me.

The first four applicants went into the interview room separately and came out within five or ten minutes with what looked like a refusal note. The letter in their hands when they came out of the room had a prominent red stamp across the middle. The same happened to the two smartly dressed businessmen who went in right after. Then came the turn of the lady requiring medical attention. Her interview lasted a little longer and she came out with a smile and beaming with joy. "I am going to England", she murmured as she walked passed me.

"I am happy for you", I responded.

Lastly, it was my turn. I was confident and ready, but very nervous as I had just witnessed six refusals. The odds were really not in my favour, but I remained composed. As I sat there by myself waiting to be invited in, I heard the interview room's door being locked from the inside. The lady at the counter informed me that the visa interviews had ended for the day. I had to re-schedule, she said. I walked up to the counter and explained that I had been waiting for this moment for eight weeks and that it was unfair to expect me to wait any longer.

With a look of embarrassment, she asked for my appointment card. I handed it to her and after checking it, she asked me to give her my passport. She then asked me to leave and to come back at 16:00 on the same day. I could not risk being late so I decided to stay just outside the High Commission and used the time to practice my questions and adjust my answers.

I was by myself in the front yard pacing up and down and repeating my answers until my mouth was completely dry. My fate was going to be decided on that day and I allowed nothing to disturb my focus. I had not eaten all day and although I felt a bit dizzy, I kept the faith, knowing that there was food waiting for me in England. But I had to get there first.

I returned to the reception on time and at about 16:15, someone called my name from behind the desk. My heart skipped a beat. I came forth and realised that it was a different person. The lady I dealt with was no longer there. The man that I was seeing for the first time was smartly dressed and wore a pair of glasses that hung just above the tip of his nose. With no eye contact, he slowly slipped a bunch of papers through the hatch.

With shaky hands, I pulled them out and noticed that they were the documents that I had submitted on my first visit. At this stage, I was unsure what to think. I was overwhelmed and felt as though my heart was going to burst out of my chest. I felt a drop of cold sweat on my forehead when I saw my passport in the hand of the attendant. He slipped a piece of paper towards me and asked me to sign on the dotted line at the bottom.

I did not even bother to scan the information on that paper. I signed as instructed and slipped it right back. Then, without any hints or clues in his facial expressions, he dropped my passport in the hatch and wished me a good day and said nothing more. I found out a few minutes later that I had been granted a twelve months student visa. I was on my way to Europe, once again and I did not even have to explain myself. This time, I was going to begin a new life and create a better future for myself. Although it was the outcome I hoped for, it still felt like a miracle. I could not find words to explain to myself what had just happened. I was going to London - United Kingdom.

It felt amazing, a second chance to do something meaningful with my life, away from the chaos in my family. I returned home the same day but before the four hours journey, I went to a small shop and bought some sellotape. I put my passport in an A5 envelop and secured it against my chest with the sticky tape . Then I dropped my shirt above it just in case I fell asleep during the journey. I could not risk having this passport stolen and I know that the precautionary measure that I took was extreme but it was worth it. I got home safe with my document.

I told my father what had happened and he was not as pleased to hear as I hoped he would be. It occurred to me that he did not really believe that my application would be successful. He realised that it was time to spend a considerable amount of money and suddenly got a bit distant for a couple of days. But he could not back out of his commitment. I had not given him any excuse to dash my plans.

I went ahead and booked my flight to London that same week and brought him the flight confirmation. It was a bit difficult for him to look away as I had done everything with little involvement on his part. In the evening of Sunday 18th of November 2001, just four days after I was issued my visa, I was boarding an Air France flight to Heathrow via Paris.

On the day of my departure, I told everybody that I did not want to be accompanied to the airport as usual. I felt like it was time for me to face my own fate alone. My father understood that and did not insist. My mother cooked a large meal for the whole family and we had a very small farewell dinner at home. Then, I left home in a taxi and my flight took off less than two hours later.

At that time of the year, the weather is warm and dry in Cameroon and I was dressed with that tropical climate in mind, knowing very little about the winter weather in Europe and especially in the United Kingdom. So, when the plane landed at Heathrow London, I had a shock. If you, my reader, have seen the movie *Cool Runnings*, there is a scene when the young men, coming to take part in a competition arrived in the United States from the West Indies for the first time. They found themselves in a blowing cold wind when they landed and refused to leave the airport because of the harsh cold feeling that they were experiencing for the first time.

That was exactly what happened when I arrived in London on that Tuesday morning. The clothes I had on were made of very light materials and made no difference in the English cold. I looked around and noticed that everybody was dressed in clothes that were adapted to low temperatures. I was shivering.

All of my previous visits on the old continent had always been during the summer months. But not this time. Also, unlike my previous visits, nobody was waiting for me at the airport when I arrived. I had the home address of my host family in Cambridge scribbled on a piece of paper and I had no idea how far Cambridge was from London. Google Maps was still a thing of the future at that point.

I asked around and a very nice man stopped and pointed me to the National Express coach ticket office. I had a few hundred US Dollars with me and had to change them into Great British Pound before making any purchase. The pound was, and still is, the strongest currency in the world and after the conversion, I was left with a lot less money. I bought a one-way ticket to Cambridge at a cost of 20 pound. The journey lasted a little over three hours.

Once we arrived in Cambridge and got off the coach, I noticed that bicycles were parked at every corner. I waved down a taxi and when I got in, the old bald driver said nothing to me. I showed him the address and we drove off. As I felt uneasy with his silence, I asked him to turn the radio on. He did. I looked outside the window and saw a lot more bicycles being ridden by people of all ages and races. The majority of people on the streets were young and that made me realise that I was in the right place.

At the address, I paid the driver, got off and dragged my bags to door number thirteen on Ramsey road. I knocked three times and waited. A few seconds later Sandy, the lady of the house, opened the door and with a big smile, she gave me a warm hug and invited me in. I took my shoes off before stepping on the black thin rug on the living room floor.

Hussain, her Lebanon-born husband, was slumped on the sofa watching television. He got up, shook my hand and sat back down without saying a word. His lovely English wife showed me around the house, starting from the kitchen, then the bathroom and finally, my small but cosy bedroom. I read a few printed house rules before calling my school to inform that I had arrived and would be in class the next day.

It was around 16:00 when my host family and I sat at the table for dinner and we took the opportunity to get to know more about each other. Sandy told me everything about her native Cambridge and all the wonderful sights that I was going to discover during my stay. She talked about the museums, the big churches and cathedrals, the clubs and pubs, the shopping centre and the many like-minded students that I would be meeting.

Hussain did not say much, but when he did, it was to make me laugh. He was witty and told jokes that I didn't understand at the time but which made sense much later as I got more familiar with the British accent and sense of humour. I noticed that he had very few teeth; which is probably why he said nothing when we first met.

I had an early night on that first day with my host family. I went to bed thinking of everything that had happened a few days earlier, my visa interview or lack-thereof, the trip's preparation, my family, the home that I left and everything in between. There seemed to have been too many metamorphoses in my short years. But I was looking forward to whatever else the future held for me.

The following morning, after breakfast, Sandy gave me a map and showed me the quickest way to get to the New School of English. After about twenty minutes walk, I arrived there and was warmly welcomed by the admin staff. I was invited to sign a few forms, fill in a couple of questionnaires and my first day at school began. Teachers were great professionals and delivered their lectures with a lot of tactfulness and patience. One of them stood out for me as I recall. His name was Trevor Bryant. I believe that he might have been a good stand-up comedian if he hadn't been a teacher. His quirky and eccentric teaching style made him so much fun to be around. He was easy to understand and the whole class loved his relaxed approach.

I was the only Sub-Saharan African in my class and possibly the only one in the whole school at that time, if I remember correctly. Most students came from Western Europe and the Middle-East. There were a few students from Japan and South Korea. One girl caught my eye on my second day . Her name was Olivia. She was twenty years old and came from Switzerland.

I saw her for the first time in the basement where all the students hung out during breaks to play snooker and watch television. She was sitting with her friend, also from Switzerland, chatting away when our eyes met. I knew then, that this beautiful slim girl and I would get along just fine. Initially, I simply introduced myself to her and when she responded, I felt that she was a little shy and somewhat, nervous. I did not understand why and just assumed that I had taken her breath away. I believed that she found me irresistibly attractive and was speechless. After all, I was shaven, had short hair, was smartly dressed and smelt nice.

But my physical appearance was not enough to truly win her admiration. We did not speak much during that first week as I still had a few things to get used to at school in those first few days. I bought myself a cheap secondhand bicycle to get around the city during my free time. I opened a bank account for my living expenses to be transferred into from my sponsor's account every month.

When Olivia and I spoke at the beginning of my second week, she gave me an opportunity to sweep her off her feet. She told me that she actually came from a small village in the German part of Switzerland. That is when I switched from English and started speaking to her in her native German. Her jaw dropped. I had her attention from then on. We became very close over the following weeks and met for lunch at school. She also had a bicycle and we rode around together in the city, visited museums, lakes and bars; sometimes with other students. But usually, just the two of us and I liked it that way - just the two of us.

The city of Cambridge remains, for me, the most beautiful city in the whole of England. Houses and buildings are ancient with a touch of modernity that does not completely override the nostalgia of the nineteenth century. My time there was really joyful and I was at my happiest; more so in the company of Olivia, my Swiss-German companion. She made me feel really special with her kind words. She had a way of murmuring complements in my ear. One day, we were both sitting at a bus stop on our way back from a student party when the temperature dropped below ten degrees. Although she had a coat on, I took off my jacket and used it to cover her hair as the wind picked up in velocity. She was very touched and said something that was so nice that I felt a bit uncomfortable:

"Charly, you are a really good man and I am sure that your parents are very proud of you."

I looked away. Those words reminded me where I came from. She did not know anything about my reality and it was better that way. Then I looked at her and gave a wink and she got closer and kissed me gently. When the bus finally came, she held my hand and we stepped in together. I took her back to her host family before returning to mine that night.

Six months went by quickly and it was time for Olivia to return home. The day before she left, she gave me her home number and asked me to call her the day after. When I called, her mother picked up and told me how pleased she was to hear my voice at last. Her daughter had told her everything about me, she said. Olivia came on the phone and during our short conversation, she said that I could visit her in Switzerland anytime.

Unfortunately, just as it happened with Silvia from Poland two years earlier, I also lost Olivia's number a short time after that first conversation. That was the end of another fairy tale.

School finished, things changed and life started to get hard. The good times became long lost memories as the money I had coming to my account was almost used up. It was time to get a part time job to handle the high costs of living. I had to leave my host family and get a place for myself. That was not too difficult and the rent was reasonable. But I was running out of money fast and needed some supplementary support from my father. I had not anticipated how he would react to my request for more funds.

I called when I knew he would be open to listen. He had just received a large payment for a shipment to Japan the week before. I got the information from my younger brother, his assistant. When the phone rang, he picked up and spoke absentmindedly. I told him that my situation was delicate and I needed some cash injection to move on to university to start my law degree. He listened patiently as I explained that with no money I could not go on and would be in breach of the UK immigration rules. He kept quiet and, for some reason my heart began to beat really hard. He broke his silence and said:

"Charly - I will not be sending you more money. You are an adult now. So find your own way"

Then he hung up before I could say a word.

I was crushed. I sank on my knees and cried for a few minutes. I could not believe that I had just been abandoned in a foreign land by my own father. But I could not feel sorry for myself for too long. I had to get moving. Luckily, it was summer time and the immigration rules allowed foreign students to work full-time. There were plenty of job vacancies in Cambridge at that time. I began with a motel three nights a week as a receptionist. A week or so after, a friend recommended me to a chef and I got a week-end job as a kitchen porter. Then, about a month or so after,

I found a full-time summer job at a petrol station working as cashier.

My supervisor at the station, was a man called Barry Smith. He had terrible teeth but was still my favourite type of Englishman. He was kind, funny and compassionate. He warned me to be careful with women customers at the shop and advised me not to play with or speak to children without consulting their parents. He was worried about the reaction of conservative Englishmen and women who were not familiar with coloured people like me. He said that most of them were still very closed-minded and unpredictable.

Barry was family to me.

I worked under his supervision the whole of summer 2002 and after that period, he had to cut my hours down from forty to twenty hours per week to be in line with the immigration rules. I was tired and worried all the time and not sure what to do. I attempted many times to convince my father but he was still reluctant. It even got to a point where he simply ignored my calls and messages. I had to find a way to get myself out of that delicate situation.

Cambridge was an amazing place to be for students. The social and night life reflected that in many ways. I loved to go to Thursday student-night parties. It was free to get in before 22:00 hours and the drinks were half-price throughout the night. I was a social drinker, having a maximum of two small glasses of beer mixed with a little lemonade. That was pretty much all I could handle. I was always very disciplined in my social life. It could not be any other way because socialising was really frowned upon when I was back home in Cameroon. My father locked the main gate of our family home at 20:00 hours everyday. We all had to be in doors by that time.

That worked when he was at home and not so much when he was away for days at a time. But as my siblings and I got older, being home at a reasonable time became an unconscious habit.

One evening, during a student night party, I spotted a black man on the dance floor strutting his stuff. For most of the time in Cambridge, I was the only black person around at these type of social events. But on that night, I had company. At first, I was admiring the girl he was dancing with. She was a stunning long-legged blonde wearing a black leather skirt and red high heels shoes. She knew how to move her body on the dance floor and draw attention on her svelte physique.

After a short while, I began to wonder what that man could be doing for a living and what brought him to Cambridge. I desperately needed some information that could help me resolve my predicament. At this point, my visa only had a few weeks left before it expired and if nothing was done to extend it, I would be an illegal immigrant in the United Kingdom. I waited patiently for the boring music to start and for the dance floor to be less crowded.

I walked up to the gentleman and introduced myself as Charly from Cameroon. But the music was still a bit too loud and he couldn't hear me. We moved to a quiet area and his girl excused herself and went to the toilet, giving me an opportunity to get some inspiration from someone that I was meeting for the first time.

" I am Ade from Nigeria" , he told me.

" Pleased to meet you Ade. I am Charly Ngouh and I come from Cameroon" - I said.

"Ah - Roger Milla ..." - He exclaimed.
" So what do you do for a living Ade?" - I asked.
"I am a Corporal in the British Army", he replied.
"How could that be Ade? you are Nigerian, you just told me," I asked bemused.

"Well, Nigeria is part of the Commonwealth, a former colony of Great Britain and as such , its citizens can join and serve in the British Army in the same way that British nationals do", he explained.

"Well, how interesting! I am from Cameroon and it is also part of the Commonwealth, do you think I can become a soldier in the British Army as well?", I asked with excitement.

"I can't see why not Charly. All you need to do is to check with the local Army Careers  Office right here in Cambridge. I am sure they will be able to help you out", he advised.

We spent an hour or so together that night and his girlfriend was great company too. She drunkenly told us disjointed stories about her family; which made us laugh uncontrollably. I was happy to have gone out that evening and to have had the courage to approach a stranger. I never saw or heard from Ade since that conversation. But that meeting had a significant impact on the ensuing years of my life.

# CHAPTER FOUR

# The Queen Is Calling

I left that nightclub with a sprint in my steps. I had the answer to my problem from an informed source in a place that I only visited for amusement and distraction. When I got home, the first thing I did was to turn my old computer on and get online. I found the address of the Cambridge Armed Forces Careers Office.

Before I went to bed, I sank on my knees and said a prayer. At that point in my life, I felt like life had pushed me too hard and any progress like that conversation was not taken for granted. I thanked providence for guiding my steps that evening and asked for more wisdom to navigate my way out of a situation that was literarily sucking life out of my soul.

The following day, I called the Careers Office to book an appointment with an advisor to discuss various possibilities of joining the Armed Forces as a Foreign and Commonwealth soldier. I was given a date and a time to come in a week later.

In the meantime, I researched the job opportunities offered by the British Army and I realised that there was a very selective and lengthy process to go through to become a Commissioned Officer; which was what I wanted. But I had to be realistic. My visa was about to expire and I desperately needed to be under the Army's "protection". With that in mind, I did not have the luxury of choice from the outset. I also realised that my physical fitness was not up to the standard required for the journey that I hoped to start. I looked deeper into soldiers' life and there seemed to be a lot of aspects that I did not take the time to get acquainted with. I was almost blinded by the urge to get my papers in order.

On the day of my appointment, I got to the Army Recruitment Office a little early. I was warmly welcomed and asked to take a seat in the waiting room. There were loads of pictures and posters of soldiers on the walls that conveyed different messages to visitors. Some images showed soldiers in battle looking focused and undisturbed. In the middle of the wall opposite me was a large photo of medics reassuring wounded soldiers under a large field poncho. I could also see tank drivers smiling, wearing helmets and carrying heavy weaponry.

I was very envious of those soldiers whose pictures I was gazing at. They looked very professional and their uniforms were immaculate and I could not wait to find out more. I remembered everything that had happened to me up to that point and I knew that sitting in that waiting room was another significant turning point in my life. I was still admiring the images when suddenly, a door in the corner of the room swung open and a middle-eastern looking man in military uniform came in.

"Mr. Ngouh come through please!", he said.

As I followed him in a fully air-conditioned office, a thought crept into my mind. I said to myself: " If this guy is the man in charge in this place and looks foreign, maybe I can be like him one day."

His office was colourful. A large British flag was hanging on the wall behind his chair and was surrounded by shiny silver medals. The main features in that flamboyant office were his pictures. They were everywhere and showed him in different uniforms looking elegant and glowing with contentment. A collection of trophies and miniature bronze statutes were placed on his desk next to a large mirror.

We exchanged civilities and he placed two white cups containing tea bags on the wooden table in the corner and poured in some hot water from a black kettle. He asked me to make myself comfortable and gave me the first cup with two sugars and added some honey into the second one that he kept for himself. He started our conversation with a few jokes which made me feel relaxed enough to connect with his story.

He explained that he was born in Kenya to Indian parents who brought him to the United Kingdom when he was an infant. A revelation that gave me a fuzzy feeling as it immediately created some common ground between us. The fact that he also came from Africa instantly made me trust him. I felt as if things were naturally coming together in my life again. He also told me, with a sense of pride, that he worked very hard to get to where he was and added that the world was my oyster if I was disciplined and hardworking.

I told him that being accepted in the British Army was the best thing that could happen to a young ambitious immigrant like myself. I shared my story with him without mentioning the intimate details of my family and reassured him that I had no problem giving the Army my best efforts. Our conversation was informative and very enriching.

After thirty minutes or so, I left his office and my application was passed on to a Sergeant who became my point of contact from then on. I departed that office that day with a sense of anticipation for what was yet to come. I knew that serving in one of the most respected Armed Forces in the World would change my life for the better.

When I got home, it felt very strange that I was about to take such a major step in my life without consulting anybody in my family. I thought about telling my father but I was not sure that he would even be open to listen, much less give me advice. My mother would freak out, I thought. It was all down to me alone; which was scary.

I was tempted to accept the offer of Lauren, my companion, to help me to stay in England through marriage. She was a regular customer at the petrol station where I worked and always came in with Sally, her five year old daughter who once asked me an unexpected question. The first time the little blonde-haired girl saw me, she had a look of bewilderment on her face. When I came closer to her and lowered myself to tell a joke, she asked me:

"why is your skin so dark Mister?"

Her mother panicked and rushed to apologise for her daughter's inquisitive question. I responded that I was very touched by the naïvety of a little girl who was still figuring the world out. I explained that I had a similar reaction when I saw a white person for the first time. From that moment, we became friends. Lauren was a traditional English woman who lived a very private life in a secluded community in the outskirts of Cambridge. She was separated from her partner Johnny, a wealthy computer engineer and Sally's father.

We became very close over time. She picked me up in her convertible red car very often after work and I spent many nights in her four bedroom house. She was eleven years older than me but we had a great time together. I explained my paper's predicament to her and she was happy to marry me to help me out. But I was aware of her troubles with her partner and did not want to be caught up in the middle of another feud. I had seen enough in my own family home.

I politely declined her offer and decided to start the process of joining the British Forces and to fully bear the responsibility of my decision. I was told that once I had passed the initial Basic Computer test, I would be required to bring in my passport, birth certificate, education references and police checks from Cameroon and the United Kingdom.

I successfully completed the computer test a couple of weeks later. Then I was given a date for my fitness tests in an Army Training Camp. The tests were a few weeks away and I needed to get myself ready. I was slightly overweight at the time and knew that I would not pass any of my tests if I didn't lose a few kilos. But I could not afford a gym membership. So, I decided to change my lifestyle to accommodate some regular physical exercises in the form of morning runs. I also had to work and take care of my basic financial needs at the same time. I struggled to squeeze my fitness sessions around my work schedule. As a consequence, I was tired all the time and losing the weight got even more difficult.

The next best thing in my mind was to starve myself. I skipped breakfast and had an apple or a carrot during the day. What I did not realise was that although I lost some weight every now and then, I would put it right back on as soon as I ate "normally" for a couple of days. My inability to lose weight made me question my ability to become a soldier in the British Army.

My general health started to deteriorate.

One day, I felt light-headed at work and asked for permission to take the rest of the day off to go to the hospital. The duty manager at the time, a grumpy man with a bad attitude, told me that there was no-one to take over and that I would have to finish my shift. He then said something that I believed was uncalled-for:

"Stop being a wuss." Which implied that I was weak.

Barry was away at the time and would not have used such an appalling language. I was annoyed by this lack of empathy, but I said nothing. Instead, I tried to be understanding. I could see that he was going through some personal *wars*. I could tell from the way he spoke to the other staff members. Maybe he was just being his true self; I had known him for a short period of time and was not yet accustomed to his lack of sensitivity.

The next day, I excused myself from work and took the day off to attend a medical appointment that I had booked. After some questions, saliva, temperature and blood tests, my doctor told me that there was nothing medically wrong with me and recommended that I drink a lot of alkaline fluid and rest more. I realised that I was literally killing myself with work and the worry of not losing enough weight in time for my Basic Physical Fitness Assessment (BPFA).

I was fed up with everything and although I only had about 40 days left on my student visa, I was about to give up and face the consequences of being in breach of the immigration law. I locked myself in my room and cried inconsolably. I felt that life had given me more than what I could reasonably cope with. I tried to reach Lauren just to hear a familiar voice but her phone was off.

After I had cried for sometime, I started laughing. I looked around me and realised that although times were hard, all was not lost. The fact that I cried so much turned out to be a form of therapy because it seemed as if poison had exited my body. I pulled myself together and became very calm and positive. But I later found out that it was too soon to get my hopes up. I got a call from the  recruitment office a couple of days later asking me to come in.

I had a feeling that something was wrong and I was right. My medical tests had come back and there was bad news. I had a heart murmur, a subtle medical condition that could prevent me from performing certain military duties. After the recruiter explained the extend of my condition, I was devastated but was reassured that a second opinion would be sought.

Another week went by and I was invited back in. This time, it was good news, my heart condition was not as bad as initially feared. It was the best news I had had for a long time and I struggled to contain my joy. I was one step closer to my dream job and that brought some happiness to my stressful life. I was so elated that I quit my job without notice. Barry, my manager, was sad to see me go but was kind enough to wish me well for the future. He even threw a small farewell party for me after my last shift. We remained in contact for a few months after that until I eventually lost his contact details.

Now that I was getting closer to my goal of being a soldier in one of the best Armed Forces in the world, I decided to take a break. I had saved some money and with my worries gone almost overnight, it was time to replenish my spirit with new energy. I knew that the process was at an early stage and would take months to be completed. I wanted to treat myself and enjoy life a little bit for a change.

I spoke to Lauren about going away together for a short break and she told me that she could not come with me. Johnny, Sally's father, was making efforts to mend their relationship and had made some changes and was improving as a father. She was considering getting back together with him, she told me. We agreed that we should remain friends - just good friends.

After that conversation during which we ended our intimate relationship, I considered that to be a sign of a major breakthrough in my journey. My life was definitely at a turning point; my breakup with Lauren meant that I had outstayed my welcome in Cambridge and it was time to go. I booked a ticket and went to Thailand to visit Francois Le Berre, a French business partner that I got on well with during my time working for my father. I did not want to go to Cameroon because I knew that I would land in the messy situation that I left behind. I just wanted to relax and Bangkok seemed to be the perfect choice.

I needed a visa for Thailand and I got it quite easily in London. I flew from Heathrow, the busiest of the five London airports, to Istanbul in Turkey and got on a nine hour connecting flight to Bangkok. I loved every second of my time away. The food in Bangkok was a pure delight and the people were very friendly and welcoming. It was windy and very hot but I loved it.

One afternoon in April 2003, as I was hiding from the burning external Bangkok heat, I spent a few hours on the sofa and watched the start of the Iraq war on television. Francois, my French friend, jokingly told me that as soon as I get in the British Army, I would be deployed to Iraq to fight other people's war. My reply was that it would not happen because, there were too many soldiers serving and they could not all be sent to a single battlefield.

I returned to the UK from that blissful trip with only five days left on my student visa. Luckily, I had anticipated what happened with the immigration officials on my arrival. I had taken some Army admission documents with me and presented them at the point of entry. Without them, I would have been refused entry and possibly faced deportation to Cameroon. But everything went well and I was allowed in the country.

When I got home on that day, I wasted no time. I went to the Army Careers Office to hand in my passport; which was to be returned to me after the successful completion of the rigorous and lengthy army selection process.

As my application progressed, I had subsequent interviews. One of them stuck with me up to this day. That interview was about selecting my job in the Army. Although I had already decided that I wanted to become an office administrator, the sergeant in charge of my file told me that there were no vacancies in the Adjutant General' s Corps (AGC), the branch of the Army that took care of the admin. That man convinced me to join the Army Medical Corps (AMC) despite my openly expressed reluctance to deal with blood. He reassured me that I would be able to do an "in house" transfer once in the Army.

He also stressed that his priority was to get my application approved as fast as possible, which I found very flattering. But I later found out that there was another reason for his kindness. The Army had set quotas to fill because of the high level of drop outs in certain cap badges (employment roles) and the Army Medical Corps was one of those in desperate need of new blood - so to speak. The recruiter was doing his job of filling the quotas when he convinced me to go for a role that I was not keen on but reluctantly agreed to. I successfully completed my fitness test: 44 press-ups under 2 minutes, 50 sit- ups under 2 minutes, a mile and a half run under 11 mins.

On November 14th, 2003, an official admission ceremony was held to welcome the new recruits in the

British Armed Forces and I was one of nine graduates. Six others failed and needed to either re- sit the tests at later dates or reconsider their choices of joining the Forces. I had just crossed another milestone in my life as I became a British Army recruit - not quite a soldier yet.

Following my enlistment in the Army and consistent with normal practice, on November 17th, 2003, the Army requested that my passport be endorsed with: *"Exemption from Control during Service"* as a Foreign and Commonwealth Serviceman in the British Army. The request was granted on November 28th, 2003 and my Cameroonian passport was endorsed with a stamp indicating the exemption from control as follows:

*"The Holder is exempt under Section 8(4) of the Immigration Act 1971. He/She is not subject to any condition or limitation on the period of permitted stay in the United Kingdom.*

*On behalf of the Secretary of State."*

Then came the time to choose my Basic Training start date. That manipulative recruiter managed to corrupt my thinking again. The dates available had a few weeks in between and as it was November, I wanted to avoid going through the twelve weeks physical training during the winter months. I chose to start in March 2004 when the weather begins to warm up.

The recruiter assured me that the British Army had the right equipment and clothing to alleviate the effect of the winter cold. He basically told me that soldiers in the British Army did not get cold and once again, I believed him. I changed my mind and accepted to start on December 5, 2003, right in the middle of what later turned out to be the coldest Winter in fifty years in the United Kingdom.

I decided to go for it because the recruiter convinced me using a quite strong argument. He explained that all being well, I would finish my training just in time for my next birthday on March 15, 2004. I spent the three weeks prior to my Basis Training start gearing myself up for the tough training ahead. I knew that the following three months were going to be difficult on my body, my spirit and my mind but nothing prepared me well enough for what was yet to come.

# CHAPTER FIVE

# The Reality Of Being Different

I had a last meeting with my recruiters who all wished me well and reassured me that I would excel in the Army thanks to my intelligence and my proven ability to easily adapt to new environments. I had, at that point, been in the United Kingdom for only two years and spoke English very clearly with a touch of the British accent.

The officer in charge said a few heartwarming words which I was touched by. He said: "Unlike many young men of your age who don't really know what they want for their lives, you have a clear vision for your own future and that is commendable - good luck." It was a really special moment for me and I had a feeling that I was going to achieve great success in my military career. My service number was: 2 5 1 8 0 0 6 7.

I made all the plans necessary to move out of my tiny bedroom in the contemporary house that I was living in. I had very few personal belongings and found it unnecessary to carry the excess into my new life. So, I decided to donate most of my garments to a local charity shop. I packed a medium size bag with a few items of clothing and two pairs of shoes.

My landlady, a British - Iranian woman, refused to return my 300 pound (about 230.000 FCFA) deposit because I had reported her to the local authority. She had not taken the steps to fix the kitchen and the bathroom in the house. They were both in terrible condition; water leaked from the ceiling and the boiler was causing a dangerous fire hazard. I decided not to chase her for my money. I had better things to look forward to. I let that go to move on with my life.

My Army Basic Training was going to take place at the Sir John Moore Barracks in Winchester - Hampshire in the south of England from Monday, December 8, 2003. But all of us, the new recruits, were expected to arrive and get registered the Friday before.

On December 5, 2003, I got up early with mixed feelings of fear and excitement. My recruiters had given me a one way train ticket and a journey plan. I was also told to dress smart: a shirt and tie, black trousers, black socks and well-polished black shoes.

I got on the train at Waterloo Station in London and as it set off, I wondered what I had just done. I was very nervous, my mouth was dry and despite feeling hungry, I had no appetite. My anxiety and mental restlessness grew more intense. I needed re-assurance, but I could not call to speak to anybody. No-one in my family knew what I was doing and I felt terribly lonely. I experienced an emptiness from within that I had never felt before.

As I sat on that train glancing out of the window and thinking of the future with trepidation, I noticed that there were three other young men who sat across the same carriage. They appeared to be much younger than me, probably teenagers, dressed as I was and cleanly shaven. The size of the bags they had, the shine on their shoes and their haircut were all indicators that we were heading to the same destination.

The train pulled up at Winchester station about an hour later and the three boys got out, dragging their bags. I followed with my own bag. We exited the station and were met by two men in uniform who asked us to line up with our belongings placed by our feet. I noticed the sharp creases on their trousers, their spotless black boots and their meticulously placed sky-blue berets. They looked exactly like the soldiers I saw in the pictures hanging on the walls of the recruitment office in Cambridge. They ticked our names on a list that they had and we joined the group that had arrived before us.

Once the names had been checked, we all climbed at the back of a military vehicle and were driven to the training barracks less than fifteen minutes away from the train station. We hadn't spoken to each other at that point. My nerves calmed down and I felt some comfort in that truck when I saw the frightened looks on other recruits' faces. They were all white and their skins had turned pink and reddish. I made sure that I did not do or say anything to draw any unwanted attention on me.

Once we signed in at the gate and got into the barracks, the truck swirled around for quite sometime and zigzagged its way to what looked like a detached house next to a large rugby pitch in the corner of the sprawling military camp . That was going to be our home for the following twelve weeks. It had a sign on it: 6 Flight.

Outside the house, was a man standing in ceremonial uniform and holding a stick. It was Sergeant Neil Morris, our flight sergeant from the Royal Air Force. He looked serious and gave me the impression that he was not someone to be on the wrong side of. Something about him, his body language and facial expression made me feel unsettled immediately.

When the truck stopped and we started to get off, the sergeant seemed very impatient.

"get off and line up quickly - hurry up!", he shouted.

We all jumped off the truck hurriedly, knocking each other over and almost causing a small stampede. Then, we stood side by side in front of the Sergeant who was, by then, flanked by Corporal Wright and Corporal Flitton.

It was cold and after a quick description in vivid details of what was expected of us, we were ordered to enter the foyer of the house. The corporals called out our names and we were split into small groups of twelve. Each corporal had a group under his responsibility for the duration of the training. As the names were read out, I waited for mine impatiently. I knew that corporal Flitton would not get the pronunciation right. So when he shouted: "recruit...hmm...ne.. ne..." and stopped, I knew it was my name and answered quickly. Everybody started laughing and I smiled awkwardly.

Some recruits had arrived early and were already unpacking in the dorms upstairs. More were yet to come as the round trips to the train station continued for a few more hours that day. Female recruits had a section in the house that male recruits were not allowed into. However, we all had the same training schedule.

I was part of Corporal Flitton's troop. He was only two years older than me and came from an Infantry regiment. I could tell that he was genuinely a very nice man. It was easy to see that acting tough didn't suit him well, he was kind and considerate. He spoke very fast and I struggled to understand him at first but got used to him soon enough.

During that first weekend, we all got to know each other in the dormitories. At the age of twenty-three, I was one of the oldest in the troop. Most of the other recruits were in their late teens. Another older member of the troop was a girl called Emma Pell. She was twenty-six years old and we got along very well during the training because she got in as much trouble as I did. I found comfort in her company and laughed with her all the time.

Most of my peers in the group came from military families and some had been in the Army Cadets for a few years prior. As a consequence, they were very knowledgeable about Basic Training, knew what to expect and seemed to be physically and mentally ready for Phase one of endurance training. I was the opposite.

Although I could speak clearly and had some good inter-personal skills, that environment was nothing like what I was used to. The discipline and rigour of army life was new to me and I had to accustom myself with everything quickly. Some of the recruits who came from the northern parts of England had very different accents that I found hard to comprehend and that was one of my challenges in the early weeks.

I got in trouble within hours of arriving at the training camp. On the Saturday, my second day in barracks, I put my hands in my pockets as I strolled around on the well-trimmed lawn. My Corporal saw me from the window of his small office and stormed out. He came to me like an angry dog and started to shout in my face. He got so close to me that his nose almost rubbed against mine and tiny drops of saliva flew from his mouth to my forehead. That was the beginning of what turned out to be a very bumpy ride.

On March 8, the following Monday, we were introduced to our Flight Commander, Captain Wylie. On the Wednesday of the same week, I said her name out loud and got the pronunciation wrong. I called her Captain "Willy"; which is another name for the male reproductive part. Before too long, I was in front of Sergeant Morris in his office. He took no account to the fact that I was from a different background. Instead, he acted towards me as if I was out to cause trouble knowingly. He screamed at me so loud that I started to break down. Although it was only a few days into the training, I was already on the sergeant's "watch list". My words and general behaviour were closely monitored.

In week 2, I was in his office again. This time for smiling too much. He reminded me that I was not there to have fun and that I was expected to look serious at all times. Also, he got very angry at me for not looking at him in the eyes as he reprimanded me. He said that it was a sign of disrespect and that I should look him right back in the eyes; which I did reluctantly.

In African culture, it is quite the opposite. If you look at your superior in the eyes while you are being reprimanded, whether it is your parent or an authority, it would be considered as a sign of a bad attitude. But of course it would be unreasonable of me to expect a senior soldier in the British Army to know anything about African traditions. With that in mind, his reaction was mainly based on his lack of knowledge of who I truly was and were I came from.

It is now probably the right time for me to emphasise that I was not being picked on or discriminated against. Although it may come across that way, I was being treated exactly the same as all the other recruits. Except that based on my history, I did not know as much as them about Basic Training and the challenges attached to it . I was the victim of my own ignorance and poor preparation. But I pushed on and trusted the process.

Training was hard, days were too long and nights, too short. The cold weather was bitter and by week 4, a few recruits had dropped out through injuries or simply back trooped for poor performance. A few more decided to leave the process altogether. I was tagging along and despite everything, I was still standing and forging forward.

In week 5, something happened that made me lose faith in humanity.

It was a Sunday and we had spent the entire day preparing for a Monday inspection by the Officer in Command. At about 17:50, we all got ready for dinner and were waiting in our dorms to be called downstairs to line up and march in formation to the cookhouse. Then I had an urge to pee. I left the dorms hurriedly to use the bathroom. Just as I finished using the toilet, Cpl Flitton, from the foyer, told us to get downstairs immediately and added that the last person will face a severe punishment.

I didn't want to be that last person with my track record. So I ran downstairs with everybody else and we all marched to the canteen.

As I started to eat, I became increasingly overwhelmed with an uneasy feeling that made me uncomfortable. Something was wrong.

The food started to taste funny, my heartbeat increased and my mouth became suddenly dry. It was a bit scary but I knew that it had nothing to do with what I was eating. The food served in the British Army goes through a very rigorous process and the quality is unquestionable - at sometimes.

I went back to the hotplate to get a small portion of apple pie that I loved, but I could not finish it. After we had eaten, we lined up outside and marched back to the house as my mind was frantically trying to figure out the reason for my discomfort. Whilst in the foyer, Corporal Flitton came up to me and was strangely very friendly.

- "how was the food recruit Ngouh?", he asked me. - "Very nice. Thank you", I replied sheepishly.

" Why is he suddenly so caring and why is he asking me and no-one else ?" I wondered.

It's only when I got to the dorms that everything made sense.

Due to the fact that I was using the toilet when I heard the call to get downstairs, I never had the chance to check and secure the locker containing all of my belongings. Unlike the other recruits who took the time to secure theirs, mine was left open and raided by the training staff. We were told on the first day that our uniforms and training kits were under our responsibility and any negligence would not be tolerated. So, with my locker exposed, the consequences were disastrous.

All my nicely ironed uniforms were tied together forming a rope, thrown out of the window and rubbing against the wet and cold outside wall. My carefully polished shoes were stepped on and ejected even further on the snow covered rugby pitch. My bed and mattress turned upside down and my sheets painted with dripping mud, my documents spread across the dormitory's floor.

My heart sank and I puked in my mouth. The other recruits found that hilarious and laughed uncontrollably. I was hurt and embarrassed but had an inspection to get ready for. I had to quickly pull everything together again to avoid a memorable punishment the next day. That night was my longest to date.

I started by hand washing what I could. Then I used the iron to dry and fix the creases. At around 22:00, the light went out. It was bedtime, but not for me. The inspection was more important than the sleep that I desperately needed. So I held the base of my torch with my mouth and carried on ironing whilst the others were asleep. I can't remember the time I stopped, but as soon as I had closed my eyes, it was time to get up again.

At 07:00, the time for the inspection, we all stood to attention by our beds and waited for the sergeant to walk in. When he got to our part of the dorms, he walked up to me and took a quick glance at my locker. It was below the expected standard and because of that, we all failed the inspection. As a consequence, the whole troop got punished and everybody was told that I was responsible for what turned out to be a miserable Monday morning. As the freezing wind blew on our wet battlefield uniforms, we were ordered to leopard crawl, run, do press-ups and sit-ups across the rugby pitch in low temperatures. The physical activities were so hard that some of us vomited and others, including me, ended up with blisters on their feet.

That single event made me want to quit the British Army. But I pulled myself together once more and kept thinking that all of the pain I was going through was leading me to a bright future. Ironically, that punishment was the best thing that ever happened to me in the Army. After that, I became very meticulous with my belongings and never allowed myself to go through that experience. I learned a valuable lesson through that punishment and became much more organised as a result. Life is the best teacher that one can have.

In week 7, I heard the sergeant say something that I found funny, but not in the way he intended. We were all lined up in ceremonial uniforms practicing some drill movements and things were not going the way he wanted. Dissatisfied with our performance, he told us that we would keep practicing until we had gotten it right regardless of how long it took or how cold it got.

He then said:

" We will stay here and by the way, I hate going to my house because my wife is ugly and very boring."

Some of the recruits chuckled at that comment but I was shocked. Although it was a very demeaning way to talk about anybody, I was surprised to hear that he actually had a wife. I found him so unlikable that I could not imagine him being married.

About halfway through the training program, things improved slightly. I went two weeks without being called into the sergeant's office to be told off. I was also becoming more in tune and up to speed with the training sessions and demands. I gradually adapted to the environment and even received praises from the training staff for my improving performance.

Then came week 8.

On the Wednesday of that week, we were taken to the swimming pool for our first lesson. We arrived at the pool and got changed into our swimming trunks and lined up to wait for instructions. The training staff asked those who could swim to raise their hands. I raised mine although I could not swim. In fact, I didn't know that I could not swim. When I was a little boy, my friends and I went to local infested ponds to do what we thought was swimming. The ponds were shallow and although we couldn't naturally float, we always kept our heads above the water by pressing our toes against the sandy bottom and moved around, half floating. That for us was swimming.

So, as I stood in front of a large modern swimming pool for the first time and watched other recruits float like dry leaves and gliding with seemingly very little effort, I truly believed that I could do the same. My turn came to step into the water. As I had signalled that I could swim, there were no restrictions as to how far I could go. So, I got in and made my way to the deep end of the pool with no hesitation, motivated by my desire to impress my peers. I kept going until my feet could no longer touch the bottom. Then I sank.

As I could not even tread water, I started struggling to stay afloat and gasped for air. The training staff were distracted and the other recruits did not realise that I was drowning. Instinctively, one recruit, a female, came to my rescue. She grabbed me by the waist and dragged me out of the pool. I thought that I was going to die that day. If that young lady had not come to my rescue, it would have been the end of my Army dream and possibly my life.

I was taken to the medical centre and luckily, I was fine. My next stop was the dreaded Sergeant's office. I had some explaining to do but I had not found a valid excuse to explain my carelessness. I planned to be open and honest and face the ensuing consequences. Surprisingly, the sergeant did not shout at me. He spoke calmly. He asked me if I was trying to hurt myself and if I was homesick. I told him that I had no reason to intentionally cause myself any injury. I explained that I had underestimated the depth of the pool and for the first time, I saw his caring side. He empathised and told me that I did not have to impress anybody and that I should remain true to myself.

That incident at the swimming pool, although unfortunate, achieved two results: firstly, It made me realise that I could not swim. Secondly, it allowed me to see the sympathetic side of a very scary man.

In week 9, we all went to the shooting ranges. It was an all day weapon manoeuvring and training and once again, I did something unthinkable.

As I was preparing for the day trip to the ranges that morning in the dorms, I fiddled with my day sack and my ear defenders fell out of it. I did not see them and went to the ranges without the most important piece of equipment for the day. When the time came to get ready for the shootings, I was the only recruit without ear defenders. I burst into tears like a little girl and the sergeant lost his temper. He screamed at me in front of everybody and said some pretty nasty things that I can no longer remember. He added that I would not last very long in the Army because I was too unpredictable. These were harsh words, but considering the circumstances, they were justified.

The staff had a spare pair of ear defenders that I borrowed and, fortunately, used them to pass my ring test with ease to the amazement of all. It turned out that although I was ridiculed for being "unpredictable", I could fire and hit targets at considerable distances. Passing my tests under those circumstances made me feel really good and I smiled all the way back to camp. We officially became professional soldiers after that day and were each given a professional Army Identification Card.

During that same week, we had our final physical training tests; which I passed with ease. My strong upper body was an asset when it came to doing press-ups and sit-ups. However, I was not a fast runner and focused more on improving my strengths and did enough to pass my running test within the time limit.

In week 10, I earned the respect of the entire training staff, including the sergeant, during the battle-field tour to Belgium. We had gone there to visit the vast cemetery where soldiers were laid to rest during the two World Wars. When we got to our hotel, the concierge, a lovely French-speaking lady, was struggling to explain the hotel's terms and conditions to the group. I saw an opportunity to impress and did not think twice to get under the spot light.

I stepped forward and started to speak to the lady in French and then translated her message back to the whole group in English. Everybody looked at me as if I had just landed from a different planet. I enjoyed the bewilderment on the sergeant's face. He came up to me later that evening and said: "you are actually a very smart young man Charly - I am very impressed with the way you handled the translation earlier".

" Thank you - that means a lot to me coming from you Sergeant". I replied

" You can call me Neil. When we are away from camp, we use first names" - He added.

In truth, his compliment did nothing for me. I had already conditioned my mind to hate everything coming from that man's mouth and all the nice things he said were not going to change that. He did everything to bring out the best in me but I still hated him. In retrospect, My resentment towards him was similar to that of a child towards a disciplinarian parent.

We returned to England from Belgium by coach to get ready for our final exercise.

In week 11, We set up camp in the bushes away from the barracks and the plan was to be outdoors for three days and two nights. It was wet, slippery, very cold and difficult for all of us. But we knew that it was our last field training before the graduation ceremony. The field exercise consisted of staged attack, defence, night guards and survival tuitions.

During the exercise, it snowed so much that we had to stay longer than planned outdoors. The amount of snow on the ground prevented our normal transport from reaching us on the final day. We had to wait for bigger trucks to get us out the following day. Even nature played a part in our misery, but it was great in the end as we felt that we had pushed ourselves to the absolute limits and were proud to have done so. After the exercise and once we had been brought back to the barracks, we were all in pain with all kinds of injuries. My blisters were so bad that I thought I would never walk again. But the healing only took a couple of days, to my delight.

Week 12 was the final week. We were asked a few weeks earlier to choose the regiments and countries where we would like to be stationed. There were a few options available in the United Kingdom, Germany and Cyprus. I chose Germany without hesitating and it was approved. I was joining the administrative team of a Signal regiment in Germany: 1 United Kingdom Armoured Division And Signal Regiment (1 UK ADSR).

The Troop Sergeant told us how proud he was of us for withstanding the adversity of nature and to perform at our best. I suddenly realised that he had a heart and meant well all along. Looking back, he might have been hard at times but deep inside, he was a good man doing a great job at pushing us beyond our comfort zones.

The Basic Training was coming to an end and we were all very excited. Some of us had invited family and friends to attend our graduation. I could only think of one person that deserved to be there to see the climax of my efforts: my dear father. Although I was angry and hated him for abruptly ending his financial support for my studies, I still thought that it was the best thing he ever did for me. By being alone and having no-one to rely on, I had to find my own way in life. Despite all of my struggles and pains, I was proud of myself and understood the importance of self-reliance. I grew wiser and more ambitious.

I sent my father an invitation by fax for his visa application and he was issued a six months tourist visa by the British authorities in Cameroon. He attended the Passing Out Parade in Winchester on March 5, 2004. After the ceremony, we went to the afterparty. I introduced my father to the sergeant and they shook hands and exchanged a few words. Seeing those two men joke with each other gave me a feeling of gratitude. They had both, in different ways, made me the man that I had become.

My Father did not enjoy London very much when we left Winchester. He found it strange that people did not speak to each other on the streets and on public transport like back home. Everything was very expensive to him and he tried to haggle everywhere, even in restaurants; which I was a little embarrassed by. And of course the weather did not help. He thought it was too cold - even in March.

During his visit, someone else came into my life. Her name was Ginette and she was a distant cousin of mine. She had come from Cameroon in the year 2000 to join her husband and his three grown up children from a previous marriage. I had met her once when I was in my teenage years. But I did not know that she had moved to England. My father brought her phone number and we called and met her at the Union Jack Hotel in London. Ginette and her husband, also from Cameroon, became my family and Next Of Kin in the United Kingdom.

When my father left, I visited my new family and introduced myself to the children. Ginette was heavily pregnant and gave birth a few weeks later to a baby boy who she called Noah.

I went away to start the Phase Two training and as soon as I got to the base, I applied for an internal transfer from The Medical Corps to the Adjutant General's Corps (Office Administrator). My application was successful and I went through training to become a clerk.

# CHAPTER SIX

# The Lone Soldier

The second Phase of training lasted ten weeks and was a lot less challenging than Basic Training. Although we were still subjected to sporadical supervision during certain group activities, life was much easier for us. The training took place in Hampshire on the south coast of England and we were authorised to leave camp during downtime for recreational activities and over the weekends to visit relatives and friends.

It was like being at school. We spent most of our time in classrooms taking notes and being lectured on how the Army internal administration systems worked and how to deal with soldiers' requests, inquiries and the pre and post deployment procedures. We had lectures on military laws, the rules of engagement and studied the Geneva Convention.

I was so embarrassed about the pool incident in week eight during Phase One of Basic Training that I made the commitment to take swimming lessons . I spent an hour a day, three days a week to practice at the pool on camp with the help of a military swimming instructor and at the end of week four, I was a proud and confident swimmer.

I visited Ginette during weekends in Crawley - West Sussex. She really became my closest confidante and I shared everything with her. Her husband really liked me and was very impressed with my story up to that point. He even told me that he wished his own grown up children had the same desire and drive to succeed in life as I seemed to have.

My weekends at home in Crawley were amazing. Ginette and I went out and partied all night and on Sundays, we went for long walks and shared our secrets and ambitions for the future. I paid for the food shopping for the whole house and she cooked great traditional food for all of us. I helped where I could around the house and assisted the children with their homework.

Life was great.

I completed Phase Two training after eight weeks and qualified as a Military Clerk Class 3.

It was time to take a break over the summer of the year 2004, for a short trip to Cameroon. I wanted to spend time with my parents, siblings and friends before starting my Army adventure. When I got home, I realised that nothing had fundamentally changed . There were still some animosity between my parents but I decided not to pay too much attention to the bad vibes. I told everybody about my new career and it came as a surprise to all.

At that time, the Iraq war was making major headlines around the world with soldiers dying by the dozen each week. My mother expressed her worries that I might get sent to the battlefield soon. But again I casually dismissed that possibility by telling her, as I did to François, that she had nothing to worry about.

I returned to England after a couple of weeks and it was time to finally start work as a soldier at my first regiment in Germany. I was given an air ticket, a German rail warrant and some instructions to follow once I got to my workplace. I spent a few days with Ginette before joining my unit.

On September 30th, 2004 I was on a flight from Luton Airport in London to Hanover in Germany.

I was met by a driver who took me to my new workplace at Hammersmith Barracks in Herford, about an hour and a half away from Hannover Airport. I was expected and everything went very well. I got given the keys to my bunk and a map of the compound to help me navigate around the area. I did get lost quite a lot that weekend, trying to find my way to the cookhouse, the gym and even ended up on the wrong floors and tried to open the wrong doors. It was like being in a labyrinth.

The food in the canteen was quite decent with a wide variety to choose from. Alcohol was not allowed during meal times. But a bar was open on camp in the evenings and had all kinds of alcoholic beverages for casual recreational activities after work . I was more of a social drinker and drank the occasional beer or spirit every now and then. Nothing too heavy. This is an important point to make at this stage. The reason for this emphasis will become clear later in this chapter.

The alcoholic drinks on camp were at very low costs. I did not quite understand why so much booze was made available to professional soldiers. I abstained from visiting regularly. The behaviour of drunken soldiers was really not to my taste. So, I stayed away as much as I could.

The following Monday, two days after I arrived, I was introduced to the Administrative Detachment of the whole regiment. My uniform was impeccable and the shine on my boots was noticeable. I had made efforts to make the right first impression to my superiors and colleagues alike.

The working hours in the British Army were from 08:00 - 17:00. That was the standard, but soldiers were technically on duty for twenty four hours a day as they could be called to serve at anytime during any day. That was what we were paid for; which means that servicemen and women are, considering their hourly rate, the lowest earners in British society. But being a soldier had a lot of benefits as well: six weeks paid holiday per year, full medical coverage and much more.

On that first day at work, I was standing to attention outside the office of Warrant Officer 1 (WO1) Barnes at 07:45. He was getting changed and had locked his door from the inside.

I was expected at 08:00 precisely. In the British Army, being on time generally means five minutes before the time. I allowed a full quarter of an hour. A few minutes later, he swung his door open and asked me to come in. I marched in and stopped right in front of his desk, just as I was taught in Basic Training. He stood me at ease and asked me to sit down. He first congratulated me on successfully completing Phases One and Two of training and added that he was impressed with my good-time keeping, a good sign from a new soldier, it appeared.

After a brief introductory meeting during which he told me about the mission of the Administrative department that I was going to be part of, he put his green beret on, grabbed his stick and stood me to attention. We were going to meet the Regimental Administrative Officer (RAO) Major Lewis.

When we got to his large office, Major Lewis was very relaxed and looked much younger than he was at the age of forty three. His skin complexion was that of someone of Middle-Eastern decent. I wasn't sure if he was born in the UK or came as a child, but his accent was authentically British. I was curious to know more about his family background. But I never asked any question in relation to that. We were told in training that the only colour that mattered in the British Army was the colour of the uniform and not that of the skin.

During our first meeting, he built a rapport with me and made me feel comfortable enough to open up to him. I told him that I wanted to become an officer like him. He was very pleased to hear my ambition and told me that he would do his best to help me achieve my goal.

He added that I came across as very intelligent, spoke with clarity and passion. Just before I left, he said his door was always open if I wanted to speak to him about anything. I left his office with a feeling of pride. The struggles and difficulties that I had endured to get there were long lost memories. I had arrived at a very comfortable place and I was going to make the most of it.

I felt really happy with my accomplishments and looked forward to a bright future in an environment that I was still getting used to. I headed to the office where I was the junior clerk. I shared that working space with two senior clerks, one of whom had an authoritative working approach. I did not have a desk for myself and I was floated around doing everything that was asked of me; photocopying, filing papers in different drawers and dispatching the mail. I did not like those tasks but I knew that it was just the beginning and that things would get better over time.

During that first week I met all the Detachment members and started to really enjoy myself. I was the new soldier in the group and had to watch, listen and learn from everybody else. I knew where the red lines were drawn when it came to addressing people higher in rank; which was everybody. My polite and respectful nature made things easy for me.

The first couple of weeks were great, I sussed out the people that I believed I could form friendships with. Being part of a small detachment of administrators in a large Signal regiment of about eight hundred soldiers and officers, it was important to build strong relationships. I was going to be at the regiment for at least three years.

There was a small number of soldiers who, like myself, were not British nationals, but came from former British colonies. We were known as the Foreign and Commonwealth Soldiers. We came from the West Indies, Cameroon (myself), Ghana, Kenya, Zimbabwe, The Gambia and South Africa. These nationalities were all represented in my regiment.

Ernest Tabi, was a great guy from Ghana. He joined the Army a few months before me and was already promoted to Lance Corporal when I got to the regiment. He was also a member of the admin team and worked from a different office. He and I had a lot in common. We were the same age and actually had the same physical frame and skin tone and complexion.

He was more athletic, played football and was great on the running tracks and represented the regiment at various athletic competitions. He had a great taste in clothing and his style made him very popular with the girls in and out of the barracks. I have to admit that his success with the ladies made me a bit jealous. Although I was fluent in German, he attracted more attention when we went on a night out in Herford town.

But swimming was the one thing I beat him at. He could not swim and when we got to the local swimming pool together on weekends, he ran around with the kids in the shallow end while I clocked some laps in the larger pool. It felt good to be better than him at something; he seemed to be great at everything. But I looked up to him because he had more experience in the job and I could run to him for help.

Another very nice person that I met was Diane. She came from Northern Ireland and I loved her Irish accent. We became good friends quickly and I relied on her for guidance at work. She was the person I turned to for advice in the early days and our friendship was mainly work related. We joked a lot and found one another very funny.

Everything went very well during my first few weeks and although I had been told off a couple of times for forgetting to complete a minor task or for inadvertently locking a colleague in the toilets, everything was going fine. I did everything I could to fit in and be in good terms with everybody, including my immediate superior in the office who had a bad attitude. I felt that I was accepted by all and was pleased not to have caused any trouble.

Then came the night of December 4, 2004.

It was a Saturday and the Admin Department had collectively decided to have a Christmas party to celebrate the end of a very successful year and to have some fun away from the stress of work. That was scheduled ahead of the Christmas holiday period because most of us had booked time away within the following couple of weeks.

It was a fancy dress party and I struggled to find an appropriate attire for myself. I asked Tabi, my Ghanian friend and colleague, what he would be coming as. He told me that he had borrowed a wig and some red lipsticks from a female colleague and would be coming as Beyonce Knowles.

I thought to myself: "If Tabi is going to this party as a voluptuous female pop singer, maybe I should be a macho type of man". So, I went for Jonny Depp. I have no idea why I chose to be a pirate when I could have easily chosen to be JayZ or any other dominating male figure in the film and entertainment industry. I guess I did not want to send the wrong message to the group on the night and risk having pictures of me and Tabi AKA Beyonce taken sitting side by side, which we actually were.

So I went for something different and adventurous.

I bought myself a fake hat, a stupid looking moustache and a jacket with holes painted on it. But I looked nothing like Jonny Depp. My colleagues asked me who I was supposed to be and literally choked with laughter at my answer. As everyone arrived at the meeting's venue; which was in one of the offices on the ground floor of the Head Quarters, it appeared that I had great competition in the "silly costume department". One guy who was a little overweight came dressed in a skeleton costume.

The party also had a Secret Santa theme and we were all required to use our imagination to get little presents worth 10 euros or less. I got a miniature size handy craft painted in green, the colour of our beret, for the person whose name I pulled out of the hat.

At around 16:00 on that Saturday, a minivan pulled up outside the building and took us to a pre-booked oriental restaurant in Herford town centre. We got there about 20 minutes later and sat down. There was a buffet with a variety of asian fusion food waiting for us. The meal was great and alcohol was in abundant supply. There were eighteen of us in total and we exchanged gifts, told a few jokes and the evening was amazing. We addressed each other using first names as it was a social event.

At about 20:00, people started to leave to go to pubs and clubs in the small Herford town.

I was feeling bloated and dizzy because of the huge amount of food and alcohol that I had consumed;

which was very unusual for me, but pretty much common practice for everybody else around the table. Tabi did not drink alcohol that night. He had to get up early for a flight back to England to attend a leadership course starting the Monday after. He decided to leave early and I thought it might be a good idea to do the same.

As we both got up to make our way back to camp, other colleagues told me that it was too early and that they wanted to show me around town. They said that they wanted to help me discover the night life in Herford as I was the newest member of the department. I did not feel well but I needed to find an excuse to turn the offer down politely.

I was holding my secret Santa gift in my hand and tried to use it as a reason to escape the night extravaganza that I was being invited to. So, I said that I had nowhere to keep my secret Santa gift. Diane, my Irish colleague, offered to put it in her handbag. I could really not think of another excuse to escape. So I stayed - unwillingly and handed my gift, a little square red box, to Diane. She slipped it in her black leather bag. Tabi returned to camp alone. I stayed and the drinking continued. I kept drinking and eventually drank more than my body could handle. We moved around a lot that night and drank at every stop until the early hours of the morning.

At around 03:00, I found myself in a bar and as I looked around, I did not recognise the people I was surrounded by. I then realised that I had been abandoned by everybody I had started the evening with. Very intoxicated, I went to the toilet, put one finger down my throat hoping that all the poison would come out and I would be instantly lucid enough to find my way back to camp.

I vomited a lot and the smell was overwhelming. I felt a little lighter but still not in total control of my movements. I staggered to the bar counter and asked for a large glass of water to kill the lingering bitter taste in my dry mouth. The lovely German lady at the bar offered to call a taxi to take me back to camp.

A taxi pulled up and I got in with the help of the driver. When we arrived at the barracks and I got out, I handed the driver a 20 euro note and asked him to keep the change. The night guard was standing by the gate with his rifle pointing to the ground. He recognised me, waved me in and said:

" You look like you had a great time buddy, now go and have some sleep ".

I wished I had listened to his advice to go straight to my bed.

But I was too intoxicated to think straight. Instead of going to my room to get some much needed rest, I decided to check on Diane and to get my Secret Santa gift back from her.

I don't really know what I thought was in that little red box that was so important that it could not wait till the next day. I went to Diane's room in the female accommodation block. That part of the barracks was out of bounds to male soldiers. But the ban was not really enforced. I had been in her room a couple of times before but only during the day and I had always been invited for a card game or to watch a movie with other colleagues.

This time, I was not invited.

I got to her door and found it slightly open. At this stage, I could still keep myself out of trouble by simply shutting the door and returning to my own room on the other side of the barracks. My reasoning was highly impacted by the earlier activities of the evening. So, I pushed the door and entered. Diane was lying on her back in her bed half naked with the duvet only partially covering her chest.

I could see the hand bag she had during the evening placed on the cupboard next to the night lamp. My little red box was right next to the bag. At that point, I could still get away with my nightly intrusion by simply grabbing the red box and quietly leaving. But I did not. It was like I was being guided by outside forces.

I noticed that the windows had been left open and as I felt it was cold in the room, I got closer to the bed and attempted to completely cover her top half with the duvet. As I gently rolled the cover upwards, she jumped, opened her eyes and instinctively brought her both hands up towards her neck. She opened her eyes, saw me and said:

" Ah Charly - it's you".

Then, as she shut her eyes and went back to sleep, I left the room, taking with me the red box - my secret Santa gift. As I walked back to my room, I had no idea of the gravity of what I had just done. The consequences were going to be severe and their effects would instantly change the course of my Army career. But I had to wait Monday morning to find out the extend of my carelessness.

I missed breakfast that day, there was still too much poison in my body and at around 14:00, with a headache, I waited for Diane to text me. We had agreed to go for a swim that Sunday. But I heard nothing and assumed that she might still be tired and intoxicated from the night before as I was myself.

I went to the canteen in the evening to have some dinner and it was very quiet as it usually was on Sundays. Only a few soldiers were enjoying some roast pork and baked potatoes.

During that evening, while I was getting ready for work on Monday, I tried to recollect what happened and how I managed to drink so much. I also wondered who was buying me all of those drinks. I noticed that I had not spent half the money I had started the evening with and that included the taxi fare. I wondered why I could let myself be dragged into all of this unconventional social frenzy and made a commitment never to allow that to happen again. But that commitment came too late, I was already in hot waters and did not know it - yet. I had fallen prey of the saying: *"Not finishing your drink is alcohol abuse"* , commonly known in the Forces' circles.

On Monday at 08:00, I got to the office and turned the computers on. I was surprised to be by myself, it had not happened before. The senior corporal was always in first. After a while I started to feel a little discomfort in my chest. Then, suddenly, the phone rang and I jumped. I picked it up and it was Mr. Barnes, the senior soldier in the admin department. His voice was heavier than usual and he only said one sentence and hung up abruptly:

" Private Ngouh in my office now! ".

My heart skipped a beat and I was overwhelmed with fear. It was as if I had just been told about my own execution. I could not work out the reason immediately and could not think straight. But I knew that we all drank too much alcohol and that something must have happened. I started to sweat and with shaky knees, I stood in front of the mirror in the office to adjust my uniform and my beret. I made sure that the creases on my shirt were sharp and visible. But a perfect uniform was not going to change my fate as I found out a little later.

I felt sick as I started the longest journey of my life to his office; which was only a couple of minutes walk away from the one I worked in. I walked and stopped to breathe every couple of steps or so. My stomach churned even more as I finally got to my destination. I knocked on his door and announced myself. From inside, he shouted:

" Stand to attention and wait outside ".

I did just that and mentally prepared myself for a very difficult day. Some of my colleagues were walking around the corridor as I was standing to attention; which means - hands stretched on the sides, shoulders back, feet together and facing the front. About an hour or so later, two men dressed in dark grey suits entered my peripheral vision as they made their way towards me. They gently knocked on the door of the Warrant Officer and were invited in. One of the men looked familiar, but I was too shocked and confused in my own mind to remember where I had seen him before.

After a few minutes, the discipline sergeant slowly opened the door and asked me to march in. I hesitated. It felt like I was about to step into a gas chamber, but I had no choice. I marched in and stood to attention in the middle of the four men. The dreadful look on Warrant Officer Barnes's face told me a lot but not enough.

It is probably worth reminding you, the reader, that I was only ten weeks into my three year posting with this regiment.

Mr. Barnes delivered the news in simple terms:

*"Private Ngouh, a complaint has been lodged against you for sexual assault on a female soldier in her room in the early hours of December 5th. These two men are from the Military*

Police (MP) and will be investigating the matter from this moment. You do not have to say anything at this stage. Anything you do say may be held against you in the court of Law as evidence. You will be offered assistance and an adviser will guide you through the process. Do you understand?".

"Yes Sir!" - I murmured." Now, turn around, march out and wait outside." - he concluded.

When I heard those words, my heart stopped and I felt like I had just been punched in the stomach.

After the meeting where only Mr Barnes spoke, the two men asked me to take them to my room where they collected some personal items. When we got to my room, they asked me to give them the clothes I was wearing the night of the Christmas party including my underwear. I showed them the pile of my dirty laundry and they took everything.

Later that same day, a skinny bald man came to my room with two guards to collect my DNA by rubbing some cotton inside my mouth. I had still not said a word to defend myself against one of the worst accusations possible in the military. I was not sure what to think and hoped that I would wake up soon from what I thought was a nightmare.

In the evening, an interview setting was arranged and it was time for me to tell my side of the story. The military policemen invited me into a glass room, the type that I had seen in movies, to ask me some questions in relation to the incident. They began by asking me why I went to the females' block that night. My answer was simple:

"... to get my Secret Santa gift".

It appeared later that Diane, my accuser, had confirmed that she had my gift in her bag.

The next question was harder to answer:

" Why could you not wait the next day to get your gift? ".

I gave what I thought was an honest reply:

" Yes - I agree, I should have waited the next day and I regret not to have done so."

" Did you go to that room to have sex with Corporal xxxxxx that night, Private Ngouh?." - The policeman asked.

"No Sir. That has never crossed my mind. [Diane] was a good friend and I could never do anything like that to her or anybody. But I do accept that going to her room at that time was a mistake and I wish I could wind back the clock to change my own lack of judgment" - I replied.

The interview went on for an hour or so and ended with me still in shock.

Ironically, I actually never found out what that little red box contained. I never opened it and I am not even sure, to this day, what happened to it. It disappeared somehow and I really never thought of it again after the day of the incident. Everything was upside down, in and around me. I felt lonely and I blamed myself but there was nothing I could do to escape the situation that I had created for myself.

I got to my room very confused and hoped that the events of the day were segments of a bad dream. I tried to cheer myself up by having what Viktor FrankI calls *"a delusion of reprieve"* in his classic book Man's Search For Meaning. "It is a condition known in psychiatry. This is when the condemned man, immediately before his execution, gets the illusion that he might be reprieved at the very last minute" - says Viktor.

Despite all of this, I was still expected to carry on as normal in my daily duties as a clerk. But nothing was normal for me from that point. My colleagues were all told, separately, not to discuss the matter during or off work. They all made the effort to ignore the subject. But that did nothing to soothe my embarrassment and discomfort. I preferred to be alone in my room but I had to work and keep my inner turmoil under control.

I saw my accuser everyday, working and sometimes even laughing with her at work. Everyone pretended that everything was fine every day for the following four months after the complaint. I had various interviews with senior officers but mainly relating to my performance at work; which had suffered as a result of my unfocused mental state. The Regimental Administrative Officer, Major Lewis, had some compassion and spoke to me every now and then.

I seriously considered going AWOL (Absence WithOut Leave), but that would have made matters worse. I could not use sickness as an excuse not to come to work. Soldiers don't just call in sick in the Army. There was a sickbay on camp and anybody not feeling well had to report there to get treatment and a sick note to justify any absence from work.

Times were really hard for me at that point and I regretted ever joining the Army. My career was about to be cut short and I was facing the possibility of spending many years in a civilian prison. I was so scared that I did not think about my own defence. I also never mentioned the incident to Ginette, although we had regular phone conversations. I endured the discomfort of my predicament but kept it to myself.

I was offered the opportunity to move to a different camp, not far from Hammersmith Barracks. But I turned it down for two reasons: The first was that I knew it would not alter the course of the investigation. The second reason was that if I had accepted, I thought it would have meant that I was guilty of what I was accused of. So, I stayed at Hammersmith Barracks.

I was casually offered an adviser, someone to help me formulate my answers to the police. But I did not think that I needed one. I thought that, sooner or later, the case would be dropped. I was innocent. But I had not fully comprehended the seriousness of the circumstances surrounding the accusation.

Normally, I should have been given an adviser and not asked if I wanted one. So instead of seeking advice, I ran my mouth, kept talking until I said enough of the wrong things to seal my own fate. I realised that the police kept asking me the same questions in different formulations. But I, unknowingly, gave them different incriminating answers to the same questions.

During the time of the investigation, I was not happy with myself for making poor decisions and neither was I satisfied with the way everything was handled by my regiment. I became angry and resentful. I found the opportunity to bring that anger out by taking part in the yearly inter-regimental boxing competition. The physical training staff had sent a memo around the camp looking for volunteers to take part in the boxing competition. They did not need to ask me twice. I joined the boxing team for very personal reasons and I trained hard to keep my mind occupied. Training took me away from the office for several hours each day and I liked that.

On the evening of the competition, everyone was dressed in ceremonial uniform to watch some brutal bouts. When my turn came, in the middle of the evening, I was prepared to hit hard. My opponent and I punched so hard that there was blood everywhere in the ring. His blood.

Diane was in the audience with all of my other colleagues and after I had been declared the winner, they all rose, clapped and screamed my name. I looked at them all happy while I was in an emotional sadness that words could not accurately describe. At that moment, I missed my family and even cried a little. No-one could see my tears as I was sweating profusely after the three round fight. I had won the battle in the ring but I was losing the fight in my spirit.

One morning, I got a call from the disciplinary sergeant who asked me to report to his office immediately. I got there and he was surprisingly nice and even offered me a cup of tea and I sat down. He then told me that the Investigation Branch had found enough evidence in the case and that it was going to trial in the Court martial. That is when I realised that my Army career could potentially be cut short. Sexual assault is a very serious matter and the best I could hope for was jail in the Army if my defence failed to prove my innocence. Worst case scenario, I will be dishonourably discharged and thrown in a civilian jail for a minimum of five years.

I later found out that my case was sent to Court despite the lack of tangible evidence; nothing had come back from all of the forensic examinations that the Military Police had carried out. My mistake was that I tried too hard to prove my innocence instead of letting the prosecution prove my guilt. That was the result of a lack of proper supervision during the investigation stage. But it was too late, I was going to trial.

I also discovered that my regiment was more concerned with the costs involved in my case. That was further validated when I was given a lawyer to defend my case in Court. I saw my lawyer for the first time on May 25, 2005, the day of my trial. He had arrived overnight from London and we only had a few hours to prepare my defence. And that preparation actually took place in the minivan while we were on our way to Court in Osnabrück in the North West of Germany.

That preparation consisted of listening to the tapes of my various interviews during the investigation phase. The person supposed to defend me, told me that based on the language I used and the explanation that I gave on the tapes, I had no chance to walk free and that a guilty plea would be a good option. His job, he added, would be to secure the best outcome possible - a short custodial sentence with the possibility of soldiering on upon the completion of my sentence.

I did not like that arrangement and I thought that it would be fairer to fight the case and get all the evidence presented to an impartial judging panel. But I was dreading the consequences of going through a full hearing and being thrown out of the Army unceremoniously.

We got to Court and the lawyer explained the proceedings to me and stressed, again, that I had to enter a guilty plea. He pressed me by outlining the consequences of being found guilty after a lengthy trial: dishonourable discharge, disgrace and so on. It seemed that I had no choice and after all he knew better - so I thought.

The hearing started and dressed in ceremonial uniform, I marched forward to hear my fate after unwillingly entering a guilty plea. I noticed that my accuser, Diane, was not present during the hearing although she had also come to Court in a different vehicle. The prosecutor told the judge that the "victim" was too distressed and could not re-live the experience. She also did not want to face her "attacker". At that point no-one pointed out that the "attacker" had continued to share the same place of work with the "victim" for nearly five months after the incident.

That was when I realised that my battle was lost before it had begun.

I stood in the middle of the courtroom and listened to the judge as he read my sentence.

*"Private Ngouh, we took into account your guilty plea in our deliberations. It is clear from the details of this case that you breached the trust of a female colleague. Something that is absolutely not acceptable considering the circumstances. We do recognise, however, that your behaviour was out of character and we do hope that you have learned some valuable lessons in the process. We, the judging panel, do sentence you to six months detention. You will return to active duty after your sentence and we wish you all the best for the future and a successful career in the British Army"*

I was being punished because I abused the trust of a work colleague by invading her personal space without her invitation or knowledge. An act that was totally not acceptable in the British Armed Forces. The problem I had was that my offence was not formulated in those terms on paper. Instead, it said that I had "sexually assaulted" a female colleague in her room.

My lawyer had told me to expect twelve months custodial sentence. I got six months and considering that I had a clean record up to that point, I was allowed to return to full duty upon the completion of my sentence. I was going to be detained at the Military Corrective and Training Centre (MCTC) in Colchester - England.

On May 25, 2005, less than eight months after joining my first British Army Unit, I was on my way to prison. The story of my life was far from over!

# CHAPTER SEVEN

# The Military Prison

After I had been sentenced and marched out of the courtroom, I was officially a detainee and things started to happen around me that really re-enforced my new status. The guardroom staff that had taken us to Court became suddenly very formal and their behaviour towards me changed dramatically. They watched my movements and followed me around with commanding sticks. The tone of their voices became rather authoritative when they spoke to me and I immediately felt the effect of losing my freedom.

I spoke to my lawyer after the proceedings had been completed and he told me that I should be happy to have only been given six months detention; which included a two months remittance for good behaviour. What that meant was that I would only serve 2/3 (4 months) of my sentence in detention.

I never saw my lawyer again after that day. He flew back to London the same day, only a few hours after he had arrived to supposedly defend me in the Court of law. I had made his job easy with my plea and the Army spared a lot of money as a result.

From the day of my sentencing, May 25, 2005, I did not only lose my freedom, I also lost my pay. My wages were stopped immediately and I was not entitled to receive any income from the Army for the duration of my jail term.

I was driven back to camp in the back of the same van in which I was brought to Court. During the two hour journey, my guards made and received numerous calls to give our location and ETA (Estimated Time of Arrival) back to the barracks as arrangements were being made for my cell in the guardroom. All the regiment's Commissioned Officers were also informed of the Court's decision.

We arrived back to camp at around 17:30, dinnertime. I got off the van and after a brief moment, I was told to stand to attention outside. I was then marched to the canteen. It was peak time and when we got in, the place was full and with no background music of any kind, soldiers were eating in small groups, sitting around tables spread across the canteen floor.

One table was left vacant in the middle. It had three chairs around it and was reserved for me and my guards. Soldiers were enjoying large portions of steamy beef with gravy sauce for some and apple pies with custard for others while chatting away very quietly.

My guards and I got to the middle of the canteen, took our berets off and carefully placed them on our reserved table. Then, as I made my way to the hot plate, my two guards followed right behind and asked the other soldiers, waiting in line, to make way for us. I drew a lot of attention, but soldiers were really good at pretending and acted as if everything was normal. I felt humiliated and embarrassed to be paraded in front of people with whom I worked. I was the unwilling star of what seemed to be a horror movie set to me.

I got myself two pieces of garlic bread, a little bit of red bean sauce and waited for my guards to fill their plates. After they had served themselves, we all made our way back to the table and as we sat down to eat, one of them started to talk to me in a more calm and friendly manner. They knew that I had eaten very little since the morning and that sudden reassurance was, I assumed, to make me relax and eat properly. But I had lost my appetite and food tasted rancid in my dry mouth.

I could see my colleagues from the administration department sitting together and jovially talking between themselves. I could not hear what they were saying but it was hard for me to think that they were not talking about me. My situation made me very paranoid and I felt like the entire world was against me. When I looked around I saw people laughing, I immediately thought that I was the subject of their laughter. If someone had a stern look, I also assumed that I was the reason for their sternness.

It would have been much more considerate if my guards had put me in my cell and brought my meals to me in isolation. But they chose to cause me an embarrassment that I did not need by parading me in front of the whole regiment. In retrospect, it was probably a warning to the other soldiers, a way to tell them that any misconduct had serious consequences. However, I had never seen that done to anybody during my time in that regiment.

That is not to say that other soldiers did not get in trouble throughout my service in Germany, far from it.

The regiment was riddled with pending court cases of all kinds. As part of the admin team, I saw and read some very incriminating evidences on soldiers and officers alike who had committed career damaging crimes including, but not limited to, grievous bodily harm (GBH) and adultery. Those who were accused of committing any of those mischievous acts were immediately transferred to other camps, sometimes, before a formal investigation was instigated.

After the meal, my guards ordered me to walk outside and stand to attention by the main entrance. I took a deep breath with my eyes shut, hoping that I would wake up soon from what felt like a bad dream. They marched me back to the guardroom and as I started swinging my arms and stepping forward to the rhythm of the marching command: "left! right! left! right! left! right! left!", I saw Diane. She had just left the office and was heading towards the females' accommodation block.

I spotted her from a distance. Her short-cut blonde hair was tied together under a green beret. She had a clumsy walk and a flat bum that set her apart from the other females in the department. I felt no resentment towards her for my situation because, even though I believed that the punishment I was given was disproportionate to my irresponsible behaviour, it was still, my fault.

I went to my cell that night and got familiar with what was going to be my living space for a few days. Arrangements were being made for my transfer to the military prison in England. During that night, my first ever night in a prison cell, I tried to re-run the events of the day in my mind but I was too confused to think straight. I felt so lost that I tried to pray. But I did not know how to do it and was not even sure what to pray for. Then I had a migraine and drifted to sleep.

In the morning, as I was getting ready for another embarrassing round trip to the canteen for breakfast in full view of my colleagues and other soldiers, I heard a voice. It was Diane - again. She had come to the guardroom to pick up the keys to the Head Quarters. That was common practice; the clerk on duty signed the keys out from the guardroom and reported any incidence from the night before to the Officer on duty. It just so happened that she was on duty on my first morning in a cell.

On the second day, after I had gotten used to the idea of being a detainee, I became more lucid and gave the situation some further assessment. Things did not add up to me and I decided to challenge the court's decision. I asked the guardroom staff to make the discipline sergeant aware of my intention to withdraw my guilty plea and to return to Court for a full hearing.

The discipline sergeant wasted no time and came to see me in my cell after breakfast. I confirmed what I had said and added that I had a feeling that I was the victim of a blatant injustice and found my sentence extremely unforgiving for my crime. He noted my request and told me that he would be in touch with me during the course of the same day.

After I had returned from the canteen with my guards from lunch, I sat on my bed waiting to hear from the sergeant. As I was mulling over the judge's decision and the potential for a lesser sentence, a guard came in my cell and ordered me to stand up. Then, someone walked in that I had not seen or heard from since my return from Court. It was the Regimental Administrative Officer (RAO).

Major Lewis was very relaxed in his demeanour as usual and addressed me using my first name; which I found rather odd because officers normally addressed soldiers by their rank and surnames; for example in my case - Private Ngouh. Instead, in a soft tone of voice, he started the conversation using my first name:

"Charly, I heard that you want to lodge an appeal in an attempt to reverse your sentence. Is that right?", he asked.

" Yes, Sir, I do", I nervously replied.

In a slightly irritated tone, he explained:

" Well, it is your choice, but my advice is that you don't. An appeal in a case like this would amount to nothing and will waste everybody's time. I suggest you do your time in MCTC and return here a better soldier. Remember that you still have a job here and should think yourself lucky".

As a result of that "pep talk", I changed my mind and decided not to appeal.

Even in a situation of total helplessness, I was still pleasing others. I really did not want to annoy my boss because I still believed that he would help me have a great career in the Army although he never told me how.

I spent another three days in camp at the guardroom before the day finally came to make the journey to England. I left camp with two guards. We got on the road pretty early to start the eight hours journey from Herford to Colchester on a sunny, breezy and hot day. My guards turned the radio on and we listened to the British Forces Broadcasting Station (BFPS) and at some point, they asked me if I had a channel preference.

I replied, absentmindedly, that I did not mind listening to whatever was on.

I was too wary of what laid ahead and was reminiscing the good times in Cambridge; where I joined the Army and all of great memories from my previous visits in Europe in general. I wondered whether I would ever have one good experience in my life that would last long enough for me to enjoy it. Up to then, it was one failure after another. I started to question my choices and the meaning of life itself. I was only twenty five years old.

One of my guards empathised with me and said that my time in Colchester was going to be easy and life-changing. He added that he had spent a few weeks there himself in his early years as a soldier and enjoyed it a lot. I refrained from asking him what his crime was. I did not want him to get upset and use the available handcuffs on me. I simply nodded in agreement to his comments in an attempt to get some meditative silence during the journey.

He was right to a certain extend. MCTC was not the Auschwitz Concentration Camp that I had feared.

When we arrived at the gate of the prison that evening, we were welcomed by very friendly military staff members. I was asked to hand in all of my personal belongings and to sign a piece of paper on which everything was listed and verified. The two guards that I travelled with from Hammersmith Barracks signed some forms to formally hand me in the custody of the prison staff before returning to Germany the same night.

As it was after dinner time, the guards gave me a dinner pack containing two egg sandwiches, a packet of crips, a small bar of chocolate and a can of fizzy drink. I also signed for some prison items: black shoes in my size, coveralls, bed sheets, a duvet and a pillow.

After all the administrative phase was completed, I was marched to my bed space in a large dormitory. I shared the rectangular room with five other detainees; each occupying a single bed space. My room mates were members of the three services: Territorial Army (myself), Royal Airforce and Royal Navy.

I was back in Basic Training all over again.

MCTC was a huge military exercise and training compound manned by staff from the three services. The physical training was taken care of by the Army staff - mainly.

The prison had 2 wings:

A wing - This section of the prison was occupied by detainees like myself who had a sentence of twelve months or less and were due to return to normal duty on completion of their jail time. Inmates in this wing were, generally, first time offenders and had committed lower level offences ranging from minor theft to insubordination (disrespecting a Senior Non Commissioned Officer).

B wing - This section was for repeat offenders and those who had sentences above twelve months. Soldiers here were also being dishonourably discharged from the services. Detainees here had committed more serious crimes including but not limited to: Grievous Bodily Harm (GBH), Driving Under the Influence (DUI) and any type of sexual offences.

Male detainees were separated from female detainees in both wings. There were very few female detainees during my time there as I recall.

I was detained in A wing despite the "sexual" nature of my alleged offence and that raised eyebrows amongst the prison staff.

In the second week of my detention, the staff, who did not understand my presence in A wing, called me in their office, unofficially, to ask me a few questions. I gave them my version of what happened on the night of my misfortune with every detail that I could recollect. After they had looked into my file and found out that everything was solely based on the plea that I had entered, they told me that I could apply for a judiciary review.

They also added that a guilty plea was not a wise move because it would have been evident that my accuser was just as highly intoxicated as I was and could not give a believable sequence of events. Also, since she offered to keep my secret Santa gift, she was partially responsible for what happened. But they emphasised that it would be unreasonable to expect my sentence to be quashed. The best I could hope for was a sentence reduction.

I contacted my lawyer by letter the following day and, without hesitating, he applied for a judicial review of my case. After three weeks or so, I received a letter in my cell informing me that my sentence was reduced from 180 days to 112 days. I eventually only served 75 days as the rest of my sentence was remitted for good behaviour.

My time in Colchester was a humbling experience. I lived under very strict rules and was treated the same as other detainees. I was told where to go, when to go there and what to do there. My daily activities were very well structured and the outcome expected was always beyond the best. I was stretched mentally through sleep deprivation and physically through excruciating daily exercises. I lost control of my own life for a few weeks and realised that freedom was a gift and should not be taken for granted.

Every Wednesday afternoon, we were allowed to make a ten minute phone call to our friends and family. My emotions were tested when I called home. I had told no-one in my family about what I was going through, not even Ginette in Crawley. I had decided not to cause unnecessary worries to my relatives but to deal with my predicament like a responsible adult.

My mother was the person I normally spoke to during those short calls. She was always telling me about her never-ending problems with my father and sometimes, she started to cry on the phone. I was very hurt but all I could do was to try and cheer her up while wiping tears off my own face. I told her repeatedly that everything was going to be alright in the end and that she should be strong - yet I was weakened myself.

The days were long and physical training became part of our daily amusement. We set ourselves really difficult and crazy challenges like doing 300 press-ups and 300 sit-ups every day. We started the day with 50 each every morning before breakfast, 50 each before and after lunch, 50 each before and after dinner and 50 each just before bedtime.

One day, my cellmates did something that frightened the life out of me.

One of them leaned against the wall and took three deep breaths. Three others, together, applied pressure on his chest using their extended hands with the intention of starving his brain of oxygen by stopping the blood ow from this heart. They kept pressing until the skinny guy stopped reacting and then slumped over and collapsed.

As he laid on the floor unresponsive, I panicked and dropped the shoe that I was polishing and got closer. Suddenly, the guy lying on the floor by the yellow painted door took a deep breath and looked disillusioned. They all burst into laughter. I really did not see the funny side of that "game" and even found it dangerous, but I never reported it. I did not want to be a snitch.

We did not have access to the internet and were not allowed to watch television.

However, one day made the exception: July 07, 2005 - The London Bombings. A large Plasma television was installed in the foyer and we all sat in comfortable chairs watching the events unfold. Those detainees who had families in London were given access to phones to call home. The staff showed real support and understanding as we all sat to watch the unexpected terrorist attacks in the British capital.

The next day, things resumed and we were back in training all day. We did weapon, drill, swimming, health and safety training, studied military law, the rules of engagement and many other courses to hone our military skills. The main objective of MCTC was to sharpen the military skills of soldiers in detention (A wing) and not simply to lock them up as it is the case in a civilian jail.

The irony of the prison situation in Colchester at that time was that there were many soldiers in B wing who wished they were in A wing and vice versa. I found that odd but in general, that seems to be human nature; to dearly desire something we are about to lose (B wing) and to give less value to what we have (A wing).

The biggest lesson I learned through this experience was to always be grateful for what I have and never take anything for granted. I personally valued the fact that I was returning to full duty after my sentence and looking back at how far I had come, I could not afford to take my freedom for granted.

On Sundays, we went to church after breakfast to pray and sing to the Lord.

Although, I was really not interested in attending church service, I went with everyone else simply because it was the only way to get out of the communal cell on Sundays and to wear some clean civilian clothes instead of coveralls. It was also a chance to dress properly and to breathe some fresh air without doing physical training.

I earned the respect of all of the other detainees in the A wing. I helped most of them with writing letters to their girlfriends, families and lawyers. The boys were strong on their military skills but some were rather illiterate and came to me for assistance. I assisted them with handwriting and correcting their missives. Those that had difficulties reading properly knew that they could count on me.

We all had a weekly allowance of small amounts in the form of shopping vouchers. As I was a non smoker, I used my vouchers to get some cigarettes and traded them for extra minutes on the phone with detainees who smoked. I could use the extra minutes to reach my mother but also my siblings to whom I had said nothing regarding my "incarceration".

Towards the end of my time in MCTC, the staff organised a five-day adventure training trip to the Brecon Beacons in the South of Wales. Out of over four hundred detainees, only twenty five had the privilege of being part of that once-in- a life time experience. Although I was not sure about the selection criteria, I was very pleased to be one of the lucky ones. My name was called out and all of the detainees clapped and cheered. Some tapped me on the shoulders and said things like " Go and have fun, you deserve it brother". It felt good to receive some recognition from people that I barely knew but with whom I had the fortune to form circumstantial friendships.

On the day of the trip, we all had a debrief in which we were reminded that the trip was an opportunity to learn, rest and do something new. Any attempt, we were told, to escape would result in extended jail time and possibly, exclusion from the Armed Forces. In reality, all the selected inmates were in the final two weeks of their detention and no-one was stupid enough to take the risk of extending their detention by a futile attempt to run away.

The time we spent in Wales was joyful. We climbed mountains, did some kayaking, enjoyed field picnics and even mingled with the locals.

It was the highlight of my time in "detention" because I did things that I had never done before or since. We returned to MCTC exhausted after five days of an exciting adventure with loads of souvenirs in the form of pictures and happy memories.

On August 6, 2005, the day of my release, I returned to my regiment in Germany. The following report was sent to my Unit by the MCTC Commander:

" *Private Ngouh has been assessed "very good" on his training records, has improved his personal fitness and displayed much potential. It has been identified that he has shown an aptitude towards physical training and been recommended that he attend an all Arms PTI course. He has given 100% throughout and proven to be an excellent team player dis- playing fully his commitment to his military career. Assisting those [soldiers under sentence] less able within the company he interacts with ease displaying a sound understanding of others' needs.*

*His time here has been well spent; he has demonstrated personal determination and considerable effort. Providing he maintains his personal motivation and drive he should do well on his return to unit.*

*A popular member among his peers, who has assisted others less able than himself .... In conclusion this has been a very good all- round performance from a very capable soldier. Well done"* .

# CHAPTER EIGHT

# The War Is On

I got back to my regiment a different person. I was slimmer with a toned physique and well defined lean muscles. I looked as if I had been on a spa holiday in my native Africa.

A vehicle was sent to pick me up at the airport to bring me back to Hammersmith barracks, a place that I was happy to return to. I went to the Guardroom to sign in and one of the two guards who drove me to MCTC a few weeks earlier was on duty. He commented on my good slimmed-down physique and went on to say a few encouraging words:

" You see, Charly, I told you that it was going to be an enjoyable experience." "Yes - you were right but what about the stain on my military records? " - I replied.

"Well, my friend, most of us have stains on our records. Don't worry too much about      that. Do your best from now on and keep your head down" - He advised.

As I collected my personal belongings to get settled back into normal routine, I got a message to report to the RAO's office the next day. At 07:50, I was stood to attention by his office door and about five minutes later, I was invited in. Major Lewis started our meeting with a compliment. He said that I looked well.

Then he continued:

"Private Ngouh welcome back, I was very happy when I read your report from MCTC. I knew that you would do well and you proved me right. I am very proud of you. Now, I want you to know that what happened has happened and you have to put it all behind you and move on with your career. The recent events have not in anyway affected your chances of doing well in the Army. I still have faith in you and if you focus on your job, you will do very well".

As I listened to him, I had a feeling that his attempt to give me a boost was not genuine. After our conversation I felt a bit perplexed. The reality was, that time in detention affected my chances for promotion in the short to middle term. As a clerk, a private soldier normally got their first stripe within his or her first twelve months of service, though not guaranteed.

In my position and considering the circumstances, I would still get recommendations for promotion after hard work and self-discipline but the promotion itself was out of my reach for about three to five years. I looked into other soldiers' files and discipline history to come to that conclusion. As a clerk, I had access to those files.

After meeting with the RAO, I was invited for yet another "we are pleased to see you back" rhetoric by Mr. Barnes, the Warrant Officer Class 1. He also informed me that Diane was no longer part of the department and added that she was promoted and moved to a different regiment in the north of England. I was not sure what reaction he expected from me, but I said nothing.

I found out later that she was due to leave Herford anyway because

her three year commitment to the regiment had come to an end. Her departure from Hammersmith barracks was in no way linked to my return. In other words, if her time at the unit had not ran its course, I would probably have been working with her upon my release from detention.

As I was getting settled in my bunk on that first full day back, I received a visit from Tabi, my Ghanian friend and colleague. He came in my room and gave me a warm embrace and told me that he was very sorry about what happened. He also said something that I found very touching:

"Charly, God will punish all of those guys for what they did to you. People in this regiment have done a lot worse and only had a behind-the-door reprimand. Be blessed my friend, you look really good and I am very happy to see you back."

Tabi was a devoted christian.

After a couple of days, I filled in a leave application form to get out of the Army environment for a few days. My request was, at first, declined. I was told that it was too soon to have time off and that I should wait about two weeks to properly settle back in. I was then moved to a different office in the Head Quarters department where all the officers in charge of the detachment saw me everyday. Some officers took casual peeks numerous times during working hours through the window of the office I worked in. Others came in to start nonsensical conversations, apparently, to assess my mental state.

It felt like I was on suicide watch.

I was also advised to report any comment that made me feel uneasy during or after working hours. Soldiers were told not to mention or comment on "my situation".

If there was one thing about the army that I liked most, it was the respect of confidentiality. Soldiers did not say things just because they felt like saying them; there was a code of conduct that everyone abided by.

After two weeks or so, when everybody was convinced that I was not going to kill or hurt myself, my leave application was approved. I left the barracks to spend some time with the people that, I believed, really cared for me. I came back to London and stayed with Ginette in Crawley. Naturally, I said nothing about the storm that I had just come out of. All I wanted was to enjoy the calm family atmosphere at the house.

I was, at last, far away from everything military. We spoke French at home and sometimes, Bati, our dialect back home in Cameroon. We only spoke English when guests were around. I felt at peace and the food we ate, mainly traditional Cameroonian dishes, had enhanced beautiful tastes in my mouth after weeks of army prison food (heated canned beans, bread, rice, red meat and frozen vegetables).

During my prolonged absence, Ginette had given birth to a beautiful baby boy. I will call him Noah. After multiple fruitless attempts in the past, that child was her living miracle. She doted on him like only a desperate loving mother could. With a new-born in its walls, the house was even more colourful with an enhanced joyous atmosphere.

Unfortunately, I had to return to duty after my two week authorised leave elapsed; which happened rather quickly. I had to get back to the military environment that I was now struggling to feel part of.

As a junior private soldier in the detachment, nothing had significantly changed in relation to my daily tasks. On the contrary, my time in "detention" had slowed my progress as far as the technical aspect of my job was concerned. But I was much more organised, focused and never got into trouble again. I became the perfect product of the British Army; a studious soldier ready to take on new challenges within the realm of military duties.

A few months later, my Confidential Report (CR) showed that I was ready for promotion.

*"Private Ngouh has set about his work in the Unit in a confident and professional manner. He clearly enjoys the post in which he is currently employed and has adapted well to the workings and the personalities of those of cers/SNCOs and junior soldiers within the Unit. No task is ever too big and he will ask for clarification if he is unsure always giving 100% to the task given.*

*I have been very impressed with his work ethos and think he would certainly make a good Lance Corporal, ... Based on his hard work and determination, especially over the latter period of the reporting period, I agree that he is deserving of a recommendation for promotion."*

I was recommended for promotion in two subsequent reports, but never actually got the promotion for the entire time that I was in the Army. It turned out over time that I was a good soldier and had exceeded expectations and although I was not good enough for a promotion, I was the perfect candidate for something else.

One Monday morning, I received an e-mail from Captain Wilson, the Detachment Commander. It had "Urgent" as subject and the message was brief:

"Private Ngouh, report to my office immediately".

"Oh no no no not again! What have I done this time?" - I said to myself in a mild panic.

That sick feeling in my bowel set in. I started to sweat and breathe rapidly as my heartbeat increased all of a sudden. Then I thought: " hold on! Maybe I am about to receive my promotion".

I saw it happen many times before; officers created a drama around a soldier only to reveal in the end that he or she had been promoted to a higher rank.

But that carefully and promptly staged circus usually happened on a Friday and was immediately followed by an alcohol-fuelled celebration that went on until the early hours of the next day. Unfortunately, the e-mail came in on a Monday morning and I was not about to be given any news worthy of a celebration.

"Private Ngouh come in and take a seat", the Captain said when I got to his office and gently knocked on his door.

"You will be deploying to Iraq to provide administrative support to a Royal Air Force regiment on deployment at Basra International Airport. Your two week pre- deployment leave starts tomorrow.", he told me.

" Any questions?" He asked. " No Sir", I replied. " Good - If you have any, let me know by close of play today. If not, I will see you in two weeks time", he concluded.

I stood up, stood to attention, saluted and exited his office as my mind processed what I had just heard. In a one way conversation, the Captain informed me of my upcoming deployment. I could not give an opinion on whether I wanted to go on tour or if I was ready to deploy. It had already been decided; out of the thirty plus members of the detachment, I was the one chosen to go to war.

My role was to provide support to a unit already in the field and work with people that I did not know and who were not part of the Territorial Army. The Royal Air Force had very different work ethos; which were foreign to me and to which I had to adapt quickly whilst working in Iraq alongside airmen.

There was nothing I could do to opt out of the mission bestowed upon me by my hierarchy. But there was one thing I could still do to, at least, delay my deployment. So, I came back to the Captain' s office an hour or so later. His door was open and he invited me straight in.

" Sir, I would like to make a request. Would it be possible for me to take another two weeks off on top of the pre-deployment leave? I really want to go back to Cameroon to have sometime with my family before I deploy", I pleaded.

"Wait there", he said.

He left the office and consulted with Major Lewis, the Regimental Administrative Officer. He came back about twenty minutes later and made a phone call to his offsite superior and then, responded to my request:

"Right, Private Ngouh, we understand your personal circumstances and we are happy for you to see your family before deploying. Fill in a leave form and I will authorise it. We will see you in four weeks time", he concluded.

"Thank you, Sir", I uttered inaudibly as I left his office for the second time that day.

That postponement was a small victory to me. The reality though, was that I had no intention to go to Cameroon. I knew that a trip home could turn into desertion. I certainly would have been convinced by my friends and close relatives not to return to the Army to risk my young life in an unjustified conflict that had nothing to do with my own convictions.

The Iraq conflict, combined with the one raging in Afghanistan at that time, was claiming dozens of British soldiers' lives each month. My deployment was a daunting proposition but I was somewhat comforted by my role in the field; which consisted of providing administrative support and not necessarily to partake in the fight with weapons.

I came back to England and spent four weeks with Ginette and family in Crawley. I told everybody at home about my upcoming Iraq deployment and received a lot of support and encouragement. I phoned my parents back home a few times during those weeks, but hid my deployment from them. I was well aware of their own challenges and never-ending domestic quarrels and decided to protect my mother from unnecessary worries.

Noah, the new addition to the family in Crawley, was growing up well and rather quickly. I noticed that something was not quite right with him. He had behavioural abnormalities for a toddler his age. He screamed and bounced around the living room incessantly and did not seem to understand his immediate environment. No-one had a clue.

Before I returned to Germany to prepare for my deployment, I gave Ginette all of my debit and credit cards along with their respective pin numbers. I told her that I would not need money during my tour in the Middle East and encouraged her to withdraw funds from any of my accounts if she came under financial pressure during my absence.

On July, 05, 2006, day of my deployment, something happened that caused me a lot of embarrassment.

My transport was due to leave the barracks at 14:00 for Hanover Airport. I had been to the armoury a few hours earlier to sign my personal weapon out and as I could not carry it around while doing other administrative activities in relation to my deployment, I took it to the guardroom and left it in the custody of the guards.

Just before the departure time, I loaded all of my equipment in a military truck transport and jumped in the front seat next to my driver. I was booked on a civilian flight coming from Brize Norton airport (BZZ) in the north of England. The flight had a total of over two hundred soldiers from various army camps travelling to Kuwait Airport where each group boarded military aircrafts to different locations in the Middle East.

About halfway into our journey to Hannover airport that day, I suddenly had a sick feeling surging from the depth of my bowel.

Something was wrong but I could not work it out immediately. Then, a few more minutes went by before the cause of my inner discomfort became clear to me and I screamed:

"Oh no - we forgot my rifle".

The driver panicked at the sound of my voice and pulled over to set the records straight:

"We did not forget anything, YOU forgot your weapon mate" - He said while shaking his head in disbelief.

He grabbed his phone and called the guardroom to inform them that we were on our way back to get my rifle. I was on my way to war and had forgotten my weapon. I was embarrassed. I realised that not remembering to get my rifle was a sign that the extended period of rest that I was granted did not do enough to mentally prepare me for my duties in the field. My fear of the unknown was overwhelming.

When we got to the barracks, everyone laughed at me and joked about my apparent lack of focus.

We finally made it to Hanover Airport on time for the onward flight to Kuwait. We arrived in Kuwait and caught a C17 (military plane) to Basra airport where we landed in mid-morning the next day. Exhausted and breathing hot and dry air, I collected my bags and was met by James, a middle-aged man who was my guide and colleague during the early days of my tour. He showed me around and helped me to navigate the airport site that was turned into a mixed military base, mainly occupied by British forces with small detachments from Poland and the Czech Republic.

The image that I had created in my mind about my tour of duty in Iraq was inaccurate. Things were rather relaxed despite the weight of the protective gear that we carried everywhere with us and the constant threats of bombs that we dealt with.

I got to know the working mentality of the Royal Air Force and was pleasantly surprised. It was like day and night in comparison with the Army. Officers were much more approachable and did not pull rank on each other all that much. There was a sense of mutual respect between airmen and their superiors and they all addressed each other using first names, spoke politely and with courtesy.

My job was pretty simple as the private secretary to the detachment Officer in charge. I attended all the planning and strategic meetings, took notes and produced minutes every couple of days or so. I also worked three nights every two weeks as night guard with other soldiers and was equipped with a loaded weapon.

The real challenge during my time in Iraq was working at night, not because night duties were more challenging, but because it was much more difficult to sleep during the day after a night shift. The scorching heat outside made it very difficult for the high powered air conditioning units to work properly in the large tents that we used as dormitories.

Days on operation were long and hot. Nights were short and cold - generally.

Some mornings, officers and soldiers met at the improvised gymnasium for some much needed work-outs whilst drooling over Shakira shaking her buttocks in her then newly released single - *hips don't lie*. It was quite refreshing to see a woman in anything else than dusty trousers, muddy boots, no make-up, hair flying everywhere and carrying armoury; which was the case of female soldiers in the military base.

The food in the canteen was surprisingly very tasty. Meal times were longer to accommodate a much larger number of personnel and the variety of delicacies available was much wider. To this day, I don't know how fresh salad made its way into the middle of the desert but one thing I can honestly testify to is the impeccability of the logistical operation around the food preparation in general and its delivery in particular. Military chefs were assisted by cooks from India and Bangladesh mainly.

During the down times, we had outdoor parties with a very limited supply of alcohol and I was often the Disc Jockey. It was quite surprising to me to see just how chilled out the Royal Airforce staff were and to witness everybody openly discussing sensible topics like the reasons of our presence in Iraq. There seemed to be a consensus from everybody that the reasons behind the Iraq war were unfounded. But we were all on duty and these conversations evaporated into thin air.

There were also some very tense moments. I cannot say too much here with regards to the attacks that happened or our reactions to them. But in the evening of December 09th, 2006, the day that Saddam Hussein, the toppled Iraqi leader, was put to death, we had frightening mortar attacks on camp. Those resulted in the alarms being set off every quarter of an hour. Scary times!

One day, I checked my bank account online and realised that a little under 2000 Pounds had gone missing. I called Ginette in Crawley and she confirmed that she had withdrawn the money to pay the mortgage on the house for two months. She returned the money a few weeks later.

Around that time, the bird flu had broken in Africa and made major news headlines around the world. As a result of what became a major crisis, my father could no longer export parrots and other birds of prey from

Cameroon to South Africa and Pakistan as planned. The crisis frightened customers who cancelled their orders. As a result, Kamerun Aquarium, my father's company, lost money and all the investment vanished over night. Daddy became bitter and even more difficult to talk to.

I called him from Iraq when I heard of his sadness at the situation. I began by telling him where I was and what I was doing and noticed that he did not show much interest and only cared for his business and how to relaunch it. I asked him to watch his health but my efforts to make him see the bigger picture failed and I got upset. I wondered what the point was of me taking so many risks with my life if I could not have the support of my own father. But, once again, I was faced with the effects of being an adult, it was my choice to join the British Army and I had to take full responsibility for it with or without the empathy of my loved ones.

On January 10, 2007, I returned to my regiment after a drama-free and successful tour of duty in Iraq.

The following report was sent to my regiment ahead of my return:

"*Private Ngouh has enjoyed a productive detachment at Bas- rah .... His keenness to learn and to take on new challenges ensured that he quickly became a 'jack of all trades'. He is an enthusiastic individual who is happy to undertake whatever task is thrown at him, regardless of its nature. Since mid-Oct 06, [he] has been part of the Estates Flt, acting as the office [clerk]. This has been a testing period for him and one which he has worked hard to reach a competent standard. The basis of the work was alien to him and demanded attention to detail, alertness and general administrative ability. With the help and guidance of his [corporal], [he] showed that he    is capable of a good performance. His assistance with the Flt was much appreciated, allowing the [corporal] to take on many of the more strategic tasks...*

Outside of the work forum, I have been impressed at the way he has immersed himself in the social aspects of the detachment. He is a constant supporter of all functions   and voluntarily took on the task of being the DJ booth manager at the Toucan bar facility. I have received very positive feedback from the [officer in charge] of the bar, praising him for his commitment and assistance with the many functions that have *taken place. An intelligent and physically fit individual, [he] has* demonstrated that he has the ability to learn and apply. A cheerful and polite soldier, [he] uses his pleasant demeanour to achieve results. In summary, [he] can be pleased with his efforts whilst at Basra, and he returns to his unit having learnt a number of new skills."

Six months had gone quickly and a lot had changed during my absence. Most of my colleagues had moved on to other regiments and my department had welcomed new members who I had to form new relationships with. There was also a new Regimental Administrative Officer who only knew me on paper and who I met for the first time soon after my return.

Major Lewis had relocated to the UK on promotion. Major Howard, his replacement in the regiment, was a very brash and insensitive Englishman from Yorkshire in the north of England. His accent was very strange to me and he looked much older than he was, giving the impression at first glance that he had a very rough life. I never found out for sure.

I properly got to know him during the usual post-deployment interview that all soldiers returning from operations had with their respective officer in charge. Just like Major Lewis before him, he asked me what my ambitions were and I repeated myself by giving him the same "I want to be the best" utterance and just like his predecessor, he promised to do the best he could to assist me in achieving my ambitions.

In reality, I had lost the will, the desire and the drive to continue serving in the British Army at that point. I felt like all the hard work I had done to get the previous RAO to like me had gone to waste. He was gone and I was not willing to do the same for his replacement. I felt like I was lied to and played with because after all of my efforts, I was still not promoted. And all of the positive assessments I had received had not caused me to advance in my profession.

The New RAO did not help either. He jokingly said a few things that made me feel uncomfortable and out of place at times. On one occasion, he said something that re-enforced my resentment towards him and triggered my decision to move on.

Ever since my arrival in the regiment, one of the things that I have wanted to do was to learn to drive. After my return from duty in Iraq, the detachment finally granted me and two other colleagues the opportunity to take a week off work to attend driving lessons. Just before we started our intensive driving course, Major Howard asked us to come in his office for some words of encouragement. We came in and stood to attention right in front of him in his oversized office and he said:

"You are all being given time off work to get your driving licences. Make sure you pass your test at the end of the lessons. You will not be given another chance and if you fail, there will be consequences, *especially you - Private Ngouh!*."

"Wow, especially me? does that mean I am special or different?" - I was not sure what to make of his emphasis on me. But I knew, based on our history together, that he was not being sarcastic.

I took his comments seriously and used them as a strong motive to pass my test. I was determined to succeed, not because I was worried about the potential "consequences", but I wanted to see the look on the wrinkly face of that snobby and insensitive man upon hearing of my success.

So, during the driving lessons, all I could think of were his words. I was on a mission to embarrass that obnoxious officer. At the end of the week and after the test, out of the three of us from my detachment, only one person passed the driving test - *me*. The Major received the news but did nothing. There were no "consequences" in the end and the other two were simply booked on another driving test a few weeks later.

It's funny, I found, how being different can actually be used as an advantage. The important thing, as I discovered through this experience and others, is not to be bitter but to turn anger into a source of inspiration or motivation as it was my case with the driving lessons. If the Major had not made those uncalled-for comments , I probably would have failed the test like my two colleagues. I dread to think of what would have happened if the situation had been the other way around with me being the only one to fail the test.

I can honestly say that I owe my driving licence to being "singled out".

I had two weeks post-deployment leave that I spent in Crawley with Ginette and as usual, it was great. Noah, her son, had grown beyond his years and his odd behaviour had worsened. He could not utter a single word at two years old and I knew that something was definitely wrong. Ginette and her husband were not willing to take any steps to find out what the issue was.

I observed the child closely for a few days and did some research on the internet. I shockingly discovered that he had the symptoms of autism. It made me sad and I became even more attached to that poor little soul. I did not want to break the news to Ginette because I knew that she had spent years trying to have a child and this little boy embodied her success story. So, I decided not to say anything and to let her and Joseph, her husband, work it out themselves.

I returned to Germany around late February 2007 and took the decision to leave the British Army. The new RAO had made this decision easy for me, I knew that we were not going to get along and he would make my progress challenging. I could have asked for an early posting out of the regiment; which would have been granted easily because of my personal circumstances and history. But I felt a bit deflated by everything and decided to move on with my life as a civilian.

I signed off on April 1, 2007. But I had twelve months notice to serve before leaving for good.

My final confidential report reflected my decision to leave:

*"During the reporting period Private Ngouh has completed a demanding operational tour in Iraq ....*

*[He] is a well turned out, intelligent and polite serviceman. Quiet by nature, he is however very articulate and has a keen sense of humour; which he unfortunately tends to keep hidden. He is well liked and respected by all and participates in all [Adjutant General's Corps] activities. He is militarily sound and maintains a good level of fitness.*

*This has been a good year for [him]. He received praise from the [officer commanding] the unit he was attached to, for his performance whilst on Operation TELIC and then confirmed on his return to normal work that he has the ability to apply lessons learnt. He is able to work largely unsupervised and although he still needs to improve his technical knowledge, he is not afraid to ask questions and utilise the wider knowledge of [a] senior member of the Detachment.*

*Unfortunately [he] has decided that the Army is no longer for him and shortly after his return from Op TELIC, submitted his notice to terminate. He has not however let this interfere with his performance and has continued to work hard and remain motivated; as such he is deserving of a recommendation for promotion."*

On February 2, 2008, I left Germany and returned to England as a civilian after almost five years in the British Army. Unbeknown to me at the time, another war - more disheartening, was waiting for me in London.

# CHAPTER NINE

# The Pain Of Injustice

My return to England was an exciting moment. I had made plans to start my own business as an exotic pet shop owner and had in mind to apply for a business loan from my bank to get my business venture started. I looked forward to my new life after a string of unforgettable experiences in the British Armed Forces.

I was twenty eight years old and made the commitment to work hard and do whatever it took to be a millionaire in Great British Pound by the age of forty. That commitment was unquestionable in my mind and I could not foresee anything that would prevent the achievement of my unwritten goal. I stayed with Ginette and family in Crawley to cool down before entering the exciting world of business. But there was one thing I needed to get done right away.

As a Foreign and Commonwealth soldier in the British Army, I had unrestricted stay in the United Kingdom, but only for as long as I was a member of its Armed Forces. Once I left the Army, I had twenty-eight days after my discharge date to get my status changed into a lawful UK civilian resident. I wasted no time. I arranged and attended an appointment in Croydon - London at the United Kingdom Border Agency (UKBA) offices on April 14, 2008. I paid the premium one-day service fee of 950 Pounds by debit card for an application for Indefinite Leave to Remain (ILR) in the UK on the basis of my service to the country.

As I was filling out the application form, I was not sure whether to disclose the incident that had happened in the Army almost 4 years earlier. But it occurred to me that if I was not open about it, the Immigration officials could consider that as a sign of dishonesty and might hold it against me in the consideration process of my application.

So, I disclosed the "sexual offence" I had been convicted of and the 112 days sentence that I had served as a result in MCTC. I submitted my application and was advised to take a seat in the waiting room while my papers were being checked and verified by the immigration staff.

After about five hours or so, I was called into a private room and numerous questions were asked regarding the circumstances surrounding the incident that led to my trial and conviction in the Army. I openly gave all the details of the case and was told to go home and wait for a decision by post. My application, although valid, needed more inquiries done - I was told.

I was not offered a 200 Pounds refund, the difference between a postal application fee (750 Pounds) and the premium one day application fee (950 Pounds); which I had paid. I went back to Crawley a bit demoralised by the fact that I could not have my application approved on the same day. But I understood that the immigration officials were well within their right to require more time to seek the collaboration of the Army on my case.

My passport was held and from that point, although I was not technically illegal in the UK, I could not do anything with regards to my plans of starting a business. Eight weeks went by and I eventually received a letter dated June 12, 2008 informing me that my application was unsuccessful.

Here is the reason I was given in that letter:

*"In view of the fact you have failed to provide documentary evidence to confirm which paragraph of the Queens Regulations you were discharged under, the Secretary of State is not satisfied that you were discharged from HM Forces on completion of engagement and therefore qualify for indefinite leave to remain under the Immigration Rules."*

I found the reason of the refusal very odd and I looked closely into the documents that I had submitted in support of my application. I realised that the Army personnel had omitted to include the paragraph of the

Queen's Regulations that I was discharged under. The immigration officers wanted to make sure that I was not dishonourably discharged from the Army. But the Paragraph. 9.389 of The Queen's Regulations confirming that I was discharged *"by right, having given the appropriate notice"* was not in my discharge papers.

The refusal letter was sent to me with my passport enclosed, endorsed with a twenty eight day visa; which was enough time for the Army Personnel Centre (APC) in Glasgow - Scotland to confirm that I left the Army voluntarily and not dishonourably.

In retrospect, it would have been much easier for the immigration department to request that information directly from the Ministry of Defence; which in fact, was just a different department of the same government that I was employed by. But things were never that straightforward in my life, nothing ever came to me in a straight line.

It is important to note here that all I needed to do at this stage, based on the reason for refusal, was to get the information and forward it to the immigration authorities. For some reason, it took five weeks to get that very simple but important information. As a result, the immigration personnel refused to reconsider my application and asked me to submit a fresh application instead. For the second time, I had to pay a fee of 750 Pounds for my case to be processed again.

My frustration grew beyond my level of tolerance. I had done nothing wrong up to that point and my status was still not regularised. I got in contact with my former regiment to see if they could discuss my case directly with the immigration Officials. I was then informed that since I was no longer in service, it was my responsibility to get my papers in order.

To be fair, I could have actually changed my status while I was still in the Army. If I had had the foresight and the right judgement to get my papers in order before returning to civilian life, I would have saved myself many years of unnecessary frustration and pain. But I did not anticipate the drama that unfolded.

On December 05, 2008, I unwillingly submitted a second application and paid the required fee. Then, I ran out of money from my savings account after seven months of stalemate. The financial crisis happened around that time and even if things had been different, I would have struggled to get an investment from my bank. But I never got the chance to make a loan application.

Furthermore, as I got to a point where I could not make payments on my credit cards and keep up with my previous loans repayments, my creditors started to harass and pester me on the phone and with red-stripped letters through the post; which caused me a lot of stress and anxiety. I was close to a mental breakdown but I could not afford to feel sorry for myself for too long.

I got my local Member of Parliament (MP) involved and hoped that her intervention would speed up the process, but nothing changed. All she did was to get her private secretary to send letters by post to immigration officials and wait for replies that usually took weeks to arrive. No significant developments were achieved through my local representative.

Eventually, on March 13, 2009, nearly three months later, I received a response from the UKBA. My application was rejected again, but this time, the reason was different:

*"In view of the fact that you have been convicted of a sexual offence on 25 May 2005. On 19 July 2005 the Army reviewing authority varied on appeal the detention from six months to 112 days. Under the Rehabilitation of Offenders Act 1974 this conviction is not yet spent, therefore the Secretary of State is not satisfied that your character and conduct is conducive to public good."*

I was being told that I could not be allowed to remain in the United Kingdom because I was considered a danger to the public, the same public in the name of which I was sent to war - *after my offence.* In the name of the government, my former employer, the immigration officials were informing me that I was a persona non grata in the United Kingdom.

After reading that decision, I felt sick, disgusted and disheartened, all at the same time. It was too much for me to handle. And without even wanting to give it further thoughts, I told Ginette that I would be making plans to return to Cameroon. I also shared the details of my conviction with her for the first time. She listened to me attentively and although she was disappointed that I did not tell her about my detention and the circumstances around it, she vehemently condemned my defeatist attitude.

"You should put up a fight against this blatant injustice Charly. Don't give up so easily, stay here and stand up for yourself. I will support you all the way. You don't have anything to lose anyway and remember that nothing worth having comes easily. So stay and fight!" - she ranted.

Ginette had a very strong character and spoke with conviction; which gave me the moral boost and the courage that I needed to reconsider my perception of my reality. I agreed with her but at the same time I was tired with life.

I decided to stay and the first thing I did was to seek advice from my local Member of Parliament who surprisingly found the decision somewhat justified and therefore, did nothing to help me. Out of total desperation, I sent a letter to Nicholas Soames MP, one of the most powerful politicians in British politics and Grand-son of Sir Winston Churchill. As a former UK defence secretary (minister of Defence), I knew that he would be more sympathetic to my cause.

Mr. Soames showed empathy in his correspondence to me and went as far as breaching parliamentary rules by intervening for me despite the fact that I was not one of his constituents. He wrote to immigration officials, recommending that my case be looked at again, but to no avail. He wrote back to me and expressed his inability to assist me further in my tireless quest for justice. I wrote back to thank him for his understanding.

I knew that I was right and the decision to remove me from the UK was unjust. So, I kept searching. All I wanted, was for one person to look at my case from my perspective. The British government had used all its powers against me and took away my legitimate right to appeal its decision. Sir Winston Churchill once said: " never, never, never give up". So, I kept going.

I turned to the media, but got very few responses. The London- based, Black newspaper *The Voice* ran my story on their front page. *The Crawley Observer* did an interview with me and published it in their weekly paper. BBC South East did a report on my story too. But all of that low level media attention achieved - nothing!

I approached the Sun newspaper by e-mail and got someone on the phone who asked me a few questions to know more about the events surrounding my conviction four years prior. I openly told the story and the person from the paper said a few words that I will never forget:

*"Charly, I can see that you have a very strong argument, unfortunately we cannot run your story at this moment. If you had lost a limb or got injured in Iraq, your story would have more relevance. But based on what you just shared with me, I am really sorry I cannot help you on this occasion - good luck!".*

The Sun was implying that my story deserved no attention simply because I was foreign and had come back from a British war with no injury. It was a tough pill to swallow, but I did not give up. I felt that it was my duty to myself to get justice and maybe, pave the way for others in the process. I was stressed to the maximum possible, slept very little and lost a considerable amount of weight. Ginette kept her promise and continued to support me.

Luckily, although I still could not find a way out of my situation, three people came into the picture and gave me the assistance that I needed. They were, Jackie and Don, two volunteers for the Soldiers, Sailors, Airmen and Families Association (SSAFA) and Alan, a caseworker from the Royal British Legion (RBL).

I had contacted those two Forces' charities for support. After explaining my case and sharing my history with them, they locked arms with me and reinstated my faith in British society. Their assistance and personal touches gave me the strength to keep pushing for what I believed was rightfully mine; the permission to live freely in the United Kingdom. As I kept looking for a way out, good fortune came my way.

One day, as a very last resort, I walked into the now closed Immigration Advisory Service (IAS) in South London with all the written communications from different immigration officials including all of my refusal letters. My case was assessed and passed onto a caseworker - the best I could have wished for. Her name was Tori. She was a middle-aged American/French lady who saw the injustice in my papers and decided to fight my case on my behalf in the Court of Justice.

Then began a long and arduous battle that lasted for over a year.

In the meantime, as I could not earn a living in any way, The RBL gave me food vouchers every month and SSAFA, the other charity, gave me a small weekly cash allowance. Don and Jackie visited me once and sometimes twice every month to make sure that I was in good health and high spirit despite my stressful situation.

Ginette and the family in Crawley also benefited from that too as I literally covered the food shopping for the house with my vouchers.

Because I stayed in the living room and slept on a thin mattress on the floor, Ginette received free food vouchers from me, a small payback for all of her support during that difficult time. As Noah, her little boy, got older, his "condition" became more apparent. He was uncontrollably agitated at times but because I knew what the issue was, I dealt with him much better than everybody else in the house. I had taken the time to educate myself online about Autistic children and knew what to do for and with the child.

Ginette and her husband had now fully recognised that something was terribly wrong with Noah. However, instead of seeking medical and professional advice, they sought solace in Religion and God. They both joined a

London-based church where the pastor claimed to have some supernatural powers given to him by God himself to miraculously heal the sick, give sight to the blind and turn gay people, straight. All of that in the name of God.

I did some research on the pastor online and found out that he was the subject of multiple arrest warrants issued against him by the authorities in his native Kenya. He was also under investigation in the United Kingdom for money laundering and embezzlement. I informed Ginette of my findings. She was infuriated. She told me that the men of God were generally slurred online by people who had "sold their souls to the Devil" and that I should not pay attention to the lies on the internet. I was very surprised and dumbfounded by those evasive and thoughtless affirmations.

I noticed major changes in Ginette and her husband's behaviour after they joined that church. They regularly went for long nightly prayers with Noah and got home in the early hours of the morning. I could see that those prolonged church services were having an adverse effect on the child. But there was nothing I could do to help him or his parents. I also felt sad to see a desperate mother take what she believed was the best course of action to alleviate the condition of her sick child.

Gradually, the joyful home feeling that I loved vanished.

They invited me numerous times to join the church too. But I kept telling them that I was not interested. I never told them what I really thought of their new undertaking, but I saw that attending those religious gatherings gave them hope and strength to deal with a heartbreaking reality. I could see the pain in Ginette's eyes everyday as she spoke to Noah, hoping to squeeze a word out of him. Even something as simple as "mama" was impossible. The child was sick and his parents were in total denial.

One day, Ginette insisted that I should come with her to church to witness "the miracles of God" so much that I gave in. I went along with her and her husband and son. We got to Peckham, one of the most impoverished parts of London and parked the vehicle not far from a large auditorium. As we entered the church building, I saw women and children lying on the floor in unhygienic clothing. The place felt and looked more like a refugee camp than a church to me.

After an hour or so, the place was packed with an all Black audience and although I found it odd, I refrained from passing judgement. The pastor, an older man, made his entrance dressed like a head of State. He preached so hard and loud that after a while, people around me started to behave in a very strange manner. I stood there and felt as if I was in the middle of a horror movie set. A short time after, some women started undressing and rolling on the floor. The "service" went on for hours with fluctuating intensity.

At the end of what I found to be disjointed and ill-prepared sermons, the pastor asked for 100 Pounds to be put in the envelopes provided and sent forward by anybody who wanted to experience a miracle in their life. I had never seen anything like that. Ginette leaned closer to me and murmured in my ear that the only way out of my troubles was to pay the money and have a special set of incantations from the pastor who later became her mentor in the church. I was glad that I did not have any cash on me as I probably would have given it away like many people, mostly women, did.

The church ended and on our way home late that night, after six hours of witnessing one of the strangest scenes of my life, I decided to be open with Ginette and her husband. I told them that I would not be returning to their church because I did not think it was the place for me. I added that if I wanted to attend church, it would be at my own free will and not forcibly.

Joseph, the husband, stayed quiet, but Ginette had something to say:

"it's okay Charly - I understand what you are saying. There was a time in my past life when I felt the same as you do now. But that was until the Lord touched my life and called me to serve him. I have no doubt that you too will be called very soon in the house of our Lord".

On February 15, 2010, a week after my experience at her church, Ginette came back from a nightly prayer meeting with her mentor and invited me in the kitchen to tell me something very important. Suddenly, I felt a slight discomfort in my chest as I came in from the living room. She crossed her arms and delivered her message in simple terms.

"Charly, my pastor told me that the Devil is trying to get to me through someone living in my house. Since you do not like to go to church, I want you to leave immediately" - She said.

I was so shocked that I froze for a few seconds and clenched my teeth. As I stood right in front of her and my mind painfully attempting to give meaning to those soul destroying words, she extended her right arm in the cupboard above the sink and took out a piece of paper and a pen. Then she wrote the following sentence and put her signature just below:

-"I want you, Charly Ngouh, to leave my house today and if you don't, I will call the police".

Without looking at me, she left the A4 paper by the cooker and walked out of the kitchen, leaving me in disbelief. I had nowhere to go, did not have papers, nor money to sustain myself independently. The only person I trusted, even more than my parents, was throwing me out in the English winter - in the name of God.

I stood in the kitchen that day wondering what I had done to the world. It seemed that I was fighting a losing battle with life itself. Everything was against me, it appeared, and my future in the UK was hanging in the balance. On that day, with a broken heart, I left the house I called home for the last time and conditioned my mind to spend the following few months on the streets of London. I had suddenly become homeless in a country that I once put my life on the line for.

Fortunately, things did not get that bad.

I explained my predicament to Alan from the Royal British Legion and to Jackie and Don. We all met at the local McDonalds and they crafted a plan that kept me off the streets for the following nine months. Arrangements were made for me to be housed in a hostel in Eastbourne, a seaside town on the south coast of England. In the meantime, almost eighteen months since leaving the Army, my immigration case was going through the Court's system with no indication as to how long it would take.

I felt very lonely in Eastbourne. With a population of mainly Old Age Pensioners (OAP), things moved at a much slower pace in comparison to the vibrancy of London. I knew no-one and although my Hostel was close to the coast and I benefited from the fresh air blowing from the sea, I felt abandoned and betrayed. Nevertheless, I was hopeful and grateful for the support that I was receiving from the Forces charities.

Tori, my solicitor, put an amazing defence team together to work on my case and although the odds were really not in my favour, I was happy to have people by my side who saw things from my perspective. Their assistance gave a glimpse of hope and for that, I was infinitely grateful regardless of the outcome.

Before leaving the Army, I had explored the world of online dating and befriended a beautiful girl from

Cameroon. Her name was Solange and she lived in Yaoundé, the capital city of my country. I found in her the qualities of a good future wife and we began a long distance relationship.

We spent a lot of time together during my holiday from work whilst I was still in the Army and we even planned to get married. I promised her in 2008 that if we were still together seven years later, in 2015, I would walk her down the aisle. We had a serious conversation about it and agreed that it would be the right time for both of us. We wanted to use that extended period to get to know each other better, to grow wiser together and strengthen our relationship in the process.

Unfortunately, my wife-to-be had other plans.

As I walked up and down the sandy coast of Eastbourne, the thought of Solange and I starting a family one day brought joy to my heart. In my memory, I could see us together, playing with our three children in the living room of our house. But about two months after I was thrown out of my "family" home in London, I discovered that the "love of my life" was engaged to someone else. She had published pictures of herself in which she posed , cozying up to her fiancé, a man who looked significantly older than her.

I was distraught - again and hit the lowest point of my life. But I found, within myself, enough strength to speak to the only person who I knew would never walk out on me: my mother.

I called mummy and we spoke over the phone for a long time. I told her nothing about what I was experiencing, my reason for calling her was just to listen. I wanted her to tell me everything that was causing her pain and distress. She needed that call more than I did and as she spoke her heart out, I comforted her the best I could. In the process, I felt comfort within myself.

That conversation with my mother in those circumstances taught me something significant: we experience true joy when we selflessly help others through their dark moments. Since then, I have done it many times over in different situations and achieved incredible results.

I heard from Solange again four years later, in 2013. She sent me an e-mail when her marriage collapsed and we have been in very good terms since, though not romantically. We met briefly in 2016 in Paris where she lived with her estranged husband. We had an open and relaxed conversation about the past and she apologised for hurting my feelings. I forgave her and our meeting brought a healthy closure to a bitter experience. She is now in a strong and stable relationship with a French man who treats her well.

On July 9, 2010, my case was heard at the Royal Court of Justice in London. I attended the hearing and as both sides argued the case respectfully and submitted their respective evidence to an impartial immigration judge, it looked like I could win. But I had to wait another six weeks after the Court proceedings to find out.

On September 12, 2010, I received a decision from Mr. Justice Foskett that took absolutely everything into account (http://alpha. bailii.org/ew/cases/EWHC/Admin/2010/2218.html). It appeared that the government, in the level-headed analysis of the Judge, did get things wrong from the outset and failed to take into account my personal circumstances in the consideration process of my case. The judge ordered the government to reconsider my application.

On December 15, 2010, over two and and a half years after leaving the British Army, I was granted Indefinite Leave to Remain in the United Kingdom.

# CHAPTER TEN

# The Butler

was thirty years old and I was exhausted. I had no money in the bank and was not sure about where to begin to rebuild my life. But at least, I could visit my family in Cameroon and lawfully live in the United Kingdom. The forces' charities that assisted me during my ordeal offered me a return ticket home to replenish my energy and organise my future from new basis.

Before I travelled to Cameroon, Jackie and Ian - her husband - invited me to spend Christmas (2010) at their home with their three grown up daughters. It was a very pleasant experience that I had not had before or since. I felt privileged to be trusted and welcomed to have my first ever, typical British Christmas celebration in the company of an amazing family.

On Christmas eve, Jackie and her husband invited me to go with them to a church ceremony that was taking place not too far from their home. I respectfully declined by telling them that I was not feeling well. They did not insist and went without me. On that night, I was left alone in the guests' bedroom on the second floor of their family home. I reflected on recent events and felt as if I had just awoken from a bad dream but I also realised that the storm was truly over. My persistence had paid off but my energy and vigour had been depleted in the process.

On Christmas day, we all got together in the spotless kitchen of my hosts to cook a large meal. Jackie organised the cooking and allocated tasks to the rest of the family and me. We spent the morning baking cakes, frying bacon and eggs and mixing vegetables and salads into the bowls provided. We then enjoyed the succulent meal for hours during the afternoon, stopping every now and then to play boxed games and taste some very expensive wines. Ian was a wine connoisseur and had multiple bottles in his cellar.

On December 26, day after Christmas and holiday in the UK, my hosts drove me back to Eastbourne where I spent my last couple of days. It was time to get ready to go home and try to forget what had happened up to that point. Because of the media attention that my case had attracted in the UK, some patchy and inaccurate information were available online and people expressed very different opinions. Some long lost friends back home who had read about it sent me their support and encouragements. My siblings also read the story but did not explicitly share their views.

After my four week trip home, I returned to England and had to start from scratch. It was like the first time all over again as I had nothing to come back to. I stayed in a cheap hostel for three days. During that time, I looked for and found a place to live; a small bedsit in Fulham, South West London. Then, I signed on; which enabled me to get my rent covered by government assistance. As a legal resident, I was entitled to governmental help.

My next goal was to find employment. I contacted - The Sir Oswald Stoll Foundation - a veteran charity that helps ex-servicemen like myself with housing and employment training. The staff in that charity suggested that I do some work placement in the hospitality sector to get some experience; which would lead to a full time employment in that industry. I agreed and was given a front of house placement at the now closed Spice Market restaurant in Central London.

My monthly salary was equal to the UK national minimum wage and although it was not much and just about covered my monthly expenses, I was happy to be active and productive at last. The charity also arranged for an on-the-job assessment conducted by the staff from the University of East London with which they had an agreement. The assessment would end with a nationally recognised NVQ Level 3 certificate issued by the University as proof that I had become a front-of-house professional.

One Wednesday morning, my assessor could not make it to my work place to watch me cover my early shift. Her replacement, a lovely lady called Patricia, came in at around 9 am and took place not far from the welcome desk to observe my interactions with clients who had come in for breakfast and other morning refreshments.

I did my job as usual; acted natural, smiled and spoke politely. Guests felt welcome and comfortable with me and even stopped to exchange a few words under the watchful eyes of Patricia who was also taking notes on her pad as the morning unfolded. She noticed that guests, the regular ones, addressed me using my first name, shook my hand and wished me a good day and, those were my favourite ones, left me some gratuities in the form of a few coins.

At the end of a two hour observation, Patricia, impressed as she was by my performance asked me a few questions to "understand the man behind the smile" - as she put it. We were meeting each other for the first time that day and I had a good feeling. After I gave her some carefully selected information about my past, she told me that she knew someone who had an open job opportunity that she thought I might be suitable for.

I suddenly realised that the blonde-haired and petite woman could affect the trajectory of my life just as it was the case with Ade, the soldier in the British Army who I randomly met in a night club in Cambridge eight years earlier. I was excited and felt a surge of good energy coming from the depth of my soul. I gave her my phone number hurriedly and she left. But before leaving, she wished me well on the progress of my assessment. I never saw her again.

Later that afternoon, I was sitting in the upper compartment of a double decker bus on my way home when I received a phone call that filled me with joy.

"Hello! am I speaking to Charly?" - asked the soft voice on the phone.

"Oh yes Sir, Its Charly here" - I replied with excitement.

Then I froze for a second. The Irish accent of the person speaking, reminded me of Diane from the Army. But I quickly came to myself, managed to suppress the memories of that past experience and the conversation continued.

"My name is John Davoren , I am the head Butler at the Savoy Hotel in London. Can we speak for a few minutes?" - the voice asked.

"Yes - sure we can speak Sir" - I said.

"My good friend Patricia asked me to give you a call to arrange a  meeting and  see if you fit the role that I currently have open in my department at the Savoy Hotel. When  are you free  to come to my  office for a quick interview?" - Mister Davoren asked.

"I will be there tomorrow, Sir! it is my day off from my current occupation" - I replied with no hesitation.

"Charly, I appreciate your eagerness but I cannot promise to see you tomorrow. I have meetings all day; what about in a few days time? I will get back to you with a date and time.", He explained.

"Sir, I will come and wait all day at the reception if I have to and with a bit of luck, we can talk during your lunch break if you have one" - I insisted.

"Okay Charly, come in and I will see what I can do" - He replied.

And that was it.

I could not afford to let an opportunity like that slip through my fingers. Although I did not know where the Savoy Hotel was located at the time, I knew that I could easily find the address online. I had watched a program on television a few years before about it and it appeared to be a place where only people from rich and privileged background stayed.

The following day, I turned up at the Hotel, well-dressed and ready for a grilling interview. Mister Davoren was in a meeting when I arrived and I was invited to wait for him in the foyer of the five star establishment. The place was surreal and out of this world. I looked around and was mesmerised by the extravagance of the lighting and trimmings on the walls. Even the air in there seemed to have been purified with a mixture of exotic aromas. People coming in and out of the main revolving doors of the reception were stylish and dressed in what looked like expensive clothing.

As I sat there soaking up the beauty of my environment, memories of my previous waiting rooms' experiences came to me. I remembered waiting to be interviewed for my British student visa at the British High Commission in my country eleven years prior. I reminisced the feelings I had while waiting to speak to my army recruiter in Cambridge and knew then that my presence in that "fantasy world" at that moment was a sign of yet another big change in my life. My time had come to shine and I was not going to waste that opportunity.

An hour or so later, Mister Davoren finished his meeting and met me at the reception. He introduced himself and apologised for making me wait. Then, we both made our way to his cosy office on the first floor of the hotel. To my surprise, he was warm and very welcoming. We sat down and he offered me a beverage after complementing me on my jacket and tie. Then, he told me briefly about himself and what he did for the hotel.

He explained that he came from the Republic of Ireland himself in pursue of a better life in England thirty years earlier, running away from poverty and lack of opportunity in his country. He added that he had to fight his way up the chain of command in the hospitality industry before being headhunted to run the butlers' department at the Savoy right after the new owners took over six years before.

I reached down in my black leather bag and pulled out a white envelop that I handed to my future employer. He opened it to find my one page of Curriculum Vitae. He skimmed through it swiftly before throwing it in a small bin below his desk. I was a little bemused, but remained composed. Staring at me right in the face, he asked me to tell him everything there was to know about - Charly Ngouh -. That is when I truly poured my heart out and the right words kept flowing from my mind. I spoke with conviction despite my unpreparedness. He saw the desire in my passionate speech and immediately decided to take a chance on me.

Mister Davoren was a wonderful man. He took an instant liking to me from the outset, notwithstanding my lack of experience. He later used his influence at the hotel and to my surprise, I was fast tracked through the assessment process and skipped all the nonessential subsequent interviews. It appeared that he had seen in me, the right qualities for a good butler and was as keen on me as I was on getting hired.

I had no idea what a butler's job entailed and hoped to learn through trials and errors, using the qualities inherent to my unique personality. The interview process for a position as sensitive as that of a butler was highly vetted and generally took a minimum of six weeks to be completed. However, On May 28, 2012, Just two weeks after my first meeting with Mister Davoren,

I was starting my first shift at the very upmarket and sumptuous Savoy Hotel London.

I had made the decision of not letting my previous challenges affect my expectations for my own future. Instead, I focused on creating a good life for myself and to seize life's opportunities with gratitude and humility despite past events. That attitude lead me to one of the most coveted positions in the hospitality sector in the city of London.

My life changed. I had a stable job and a salary well above the national average. I moved into a clean and noiseless neighbourhood in Balham - South West London and occupied a spacious one bedroom flat. In early September 2012, I applied for British citizenship and my application was approved a few weeks later. I had realised the unthinkable by becoming a British citizen through perseverance and determination and the world was truly my oyster.

My life had come full circle. I could finally afford trips back to Cameroon up to three times a year. I earned enough to send money to my family, including my father who at that point was no longer active in business and almost destitute. Times had changed irreversibly and I felt that I had a duty of care to both my parents. I did the best I could to keep my father away from the shame and regrets of loosing his wealth through arrogance and negligence.

I loved my job despite the early shifts and late nights. It allowed me to live like a prince and to treat myself to regular long week-end trips to main land Europe and to return to Thailand where my good old French friend, François, was still living.

At work, I rubbed shoulders with the rich and the famous every working day and had inspiring conversations at every opportunity in a surreal environment. I made discoveries that took me by surprise at times; for example, it was clear to me after a while, that the really wealthy people of this world were unknown to the general public. Those individuals seemed very coy, reclusive and stayed away from the spotlight.

I also noticed that those successful men and women were no different from me, the author of this book or you, the reader. They had made different choices in their lives to succeed and what they did could be replicated. I wanted to enjoy the same success in my life as well. So, I became interested in finding out what the secret of success was. The Savoy was the perfect place to unearth the ingredients of a fulfilling life - I thought.

Our duties in the butlers' department revolved around customers' general comfort and satisfaction. Only high paying clients in suites benefited from our services. The cost per night of some of the junior suites was equal to my monthly salary at peak times and four or five times as much for the royal suite.

We welcomed guests and arranged everything related to their stay in London such as transport, visits, theatre tickets and recommended the best restaurants in the city if they wanted something different from what was offered on site. We had fully vetted child care and animal care services on call and ready for our guests . We also had inconspicuous escort services of mainly Russian women, for lonely wealthy gentlemen who needed some good-on-the-eye company for the evening. But that was never openly mentioned or discussed during our daily meetings or privately among ourselves.

Some guests drank huge amounts of alcohol and used illegal substances in the rooms. The smell was sometimes rather overwhelming. But they had the money to alleviate the consequences and the effects of their socially unacceptable behaviours. There were guests who made very strange demands. One lady, from America, asked for her room to be free from any dirt because, it seemed, she was allergic to dust. We were required to all wear gloves and cover our shoes with clean plastic bags before entering her room. I found that odd and wondered if she used the toilet at all.

Around mid-November 2012, the movie - The Expendables 2 had come out and was in cinemas across the United Kingdom. The actors of this second part of the trilogy had come to London for the premiere in one of the main London cinemas and the cast stayed at the Savoy. I got to meet some of them, including my childhood heroes: Jean Claude Van Damme and Arnold Schwarzenegger. It was a dream come true for me.

The security around Mr. Schwarzenegger was particularly tight because he was also a very high profile politician in the US and former Governor of California. But I was his butler and was allowed near him to serve him breakfast in bed.

It felt out of this world to meet those great actors and hearing them say my name when asking for assistance. The amazing thing is that I was not meant to be on duty the day I came into close contact with them. I was filling in for a colleague who had called in sick the night before. I had idolised those people since my childhood whilst playing in dusty fields in my native land. Unfortunately, that experience with my heroes will only remain in my memory. The rules of the hotel did not allow us to take pictures with guests.

Some very famous guests, like David and Victoria Beckham and many others, checked in under different names and we were not allowed to refer to them using their real names. Neither were we allowed to get star-struck or to act as if we had seen them somewhere before. It was a real cat and mouse game that we all played with perfection.

Over the months that followed, I gained a lot of knowledge about some regular guests. The department had eighteen members of staff and we all had our favourite clients. Some of the guests also had their favourite butler and Mr Davoren , the head butler, always made sure that the guests got the member of staff that they wanted; which resulted in bigger gratuities for the department. Certain guests would leave a kind note and referred to the performance of their butler during their stay in very good terms. A few of those satisfying letters made reference to me as "a polite and courteous gentleman with a bright smile."

After a year working at the hotel, I started to wonder how long I was prepared to stay in that position for and where I could go from there. Some staff members in other departments had been working for the company for thirty years plus. I did not want to be a butler for the next decades but I was struggling to see where life could take me after the Savoy.

After a few more months, I started to feel increasingly dissatisfied with my work. It had become mundane and predictable. The excitement of doing something new and different had subsided. But I could not leave yet. I had not found the secret of success and I knew that I could only get it from someone who was already successful and the Savoy was full of rich guests. However, I had to tread carefully.

There was one regular guest that I really liked. He was from Canada and always came to the hotel with his elegant wife and five-year- old son. He took a liking to me and his son whose name was also Charlie (spelled differently) enjoyed the chocolate cookies that I always placed in the room for him when I knew they were coming. I thought of the kid's needs first because I knew that he was the key to his parents' trust.

I did some research online and found out that my Canadian guest owned an IT company and had made two hundred million USD at the tender age of only thirty nine. I was very surprised as I could not have imagined this kind of fortune from such an affable and down- to-earth individual. That taught me a valuable life lesson: never judge people, whoever they are and what ever they look like. Not every rich person is flashy and standoffish.

They came back to the hotel a few times over an extended period and always left a nice letter with a hefty tip; which I shared with the rest of the department. There was an unwritten agreement amongst ourselves to put all the gratuities in a pot and to share it at the end of each month. Something that a couple of butlers in the team did not fully co- operate with and selfishly kept their own gratuities to themselves.

One day, while I was on a night shift, my moment came.

My Canadian guest had come to the hotel alone and checked into his usual suite. He ordered some food and a bottle of wine; which were brought to his room by the in-room- dinning staff. Then, whilst he was working on his laptop after his dinner, his glass slipped through his fingers and the wine spilled on the carpet. He called the butler service for assistance and I answered the phone, using the generic formula: "Butler service Charly speaking - how may I help you Sir?".

He asked for the housekeeping staff to be sent to his suite to clean up the mess that he had inadvertently made. But at that time of the night, the housekeeping staff had all gone home and the clean up was my responsibility. I went to our pantry and grabbed a cloth, a bucket of warm water and went to the suite to take care of the wet carpet. He allowed me in. I got down on my knees and started to scrub.

I was rubbing the wine's stains off the carpet when we had a conversation that completely changed my life. After a few civilities in a very friendly and relaxed atmosphere, I felt the moment was right and I asked what I believed was a risky question:

"Sir, what would you say the secret of success is?".

"Well Charly, it depends on what you understand by success and what it means to you to be successful", - he answered.

"Okay, so why is it that there are twenty fours hours in a day for all of us, yet you can afford to stay here at the Savoy and I can't? what makes the difference?", I added.

After a brief pause, he replied:

"You really don't have to be here working for this hotel. You have chosen to be here and so you are here. If you don't want to be here, then leave and do what you want to do. The reality, Charly, is that, just like most people, you are scared to do something  without the absolute guarantee that you will succeed at it. And so you stay here doing what you are comfortable with. The option of taking risks is kept away from you by your comfort. The hotel pays you reasonably well, takes care of you, your uniform and makes sure that you smell nice all day long. So, why do something else - right Charly?".

I said nothing for a few seconds and then came his next question:

"Let me ask you this Charly! How many books have you read in the last three months?". "I have not read any book, Sir" I mumbled.

"Well that is the place to start, my friend. Decide what you want to do, have or be and read the stories of those who do, are and have what you want. Then go out and do like them and everything else will take care of itself. It is that simple. I will recommend that you start by reading - Think and Grow Rich by Napoleon Hill. That book changed my life. ", he said.

"Oh my God - I have that book Sir. I bought it in 2006 after a friend recommended it to me. But I have not read it - yet. I always take it everywhere but for some reason I have never read it." I explained.

"Ah Charly! You have been sitting on a gold mine for several years. You would probably be a client in this hotel now if you had read that book the day you bought it. But don't worry, it is never too late. Read and study that book and your life will never be the same again". - He concluded.

That conversation marked the beginning of my personal development journey. I read - *Think and Grow Rich* by Napoleon Hill numerous times since and still refer back to it now. I also read - How To Win Friends And *Influence People* by Dale Carnegie. Those two books changed my perspective on life and I became a disciplined reader of various other books on different subjects, ranging from financial education to human psychology.

On October 5, 2013, I left the Savoy Hotel to share my story and to live a life of contribution. It was also the right time for me to follow my dream of becoming a public speaker; using my own story as the foundation for my message of hope to the wold.

# CHAPTER ELEVEN

# Uncertain Times

―――――――

Some time after I left this wonderfully decorated hotel, I was a little confused. I had become accustomed to reading and bought books that had personal development as their main topic. But reading alone was not going to have a huge impact on my life or even on the lives of my fellow citizens back home. I had to do something concrete. But I didn't know what to do despite the enthusiasm created in me by the knowledge that I was accumulating through reading.

I really didn't want to be an employee anymore. But I had to come face to face with my limitations caused by my lack of formal education. I hadn't gone to college and  I thought that would be a handicap for the ambitious man that I had become. So I decided to go back to school. The fees were very high and would be covered by the British taxpayer. After all, I am British.

In 2014, I enrolled on a management course at the Greenwich School of Management, a higher education provider in the South of London. The course was divided into different modules over three terms per year. I had two years of study at the end of which I would be awarded a diploma.

The campus of this institution was not very large. The first thing I noticed was the presence of a high number of black students, mostly of African origin like me. This reminded me of my visit to the revival church a few years earlier with my foster family. It was then that I began to have some doubt about my choice. In order to alleviate this negative feeling that was starting to take hold of me, I thought to myself that maybe it would be a good thing to be among those who came from the same background. We could form a big family.

In a burst of lucidity, I questioned myself and reviewed that way of thinking. Having a family away from home would be good, but that was not the reason of me being at that learning institution. I was there to be taught how to become a successful businessman. I was very studious and paid attention to the smallest of details. But very quickly, became disillusioned.

Then, a simple conversation changed everything.

One day, during the lunch break, I approached my Marketing Strategy professor to find out more about his extra-professional activities. I wanted to get an idea, however vague, of the economic health of his occupations outside of teaching. For this, I was methodical in my approach. To lighten the mood, I told him, at the start of our conversation, that I was from Cameroon, the country of Roger Mila. With sarcasm, he let me know that the president of my country had been in power for too long and that my fellow citizens should do their utmost to topple his "dictatorial regime".

"Sir, besides teaching, what else do you do for a living?" I asked him after ignoring his previous comment.

"What do you mean, young man?"

I had to rephrase my question:

"I mean... what's your business when you're not here teaching us?"

The professor adjusted what looked like medical glasses and said:

"When I am not here teaching you, I am in another establishment to provide the courses to future employers like you. My business is teaching. That's why you should tell everyone around you about this opportunity so that as many people as possible come and sign up here."

This response had the effect of a fire extinguisher on the flames of my ambition. I could not have as a reference in business a professor who had teaching as his main source of income. I expected him to tell me that he had a business with many employees and was coming just to share his entrepreneurial experiences with us.

What a disappointment!

But I was already enrolled so I had to continue attending the classes for which the fees had already been paid. It was really difficult and I felt confused and demotivated. I could skip school, but I had nothing to do with my time. My costs of living were covered by some government grants. So I had enough to meet my basic needs and my rent was paid directly to my landlord. All I had to do was to concentrate on my studies.

After the first trimester, I felt a bit betrayed by my own choice. The initial euphoria had faded and gave way to more doubt and boredom. I lived on my own and didn't have to answer to anyone. But, once again, I was  confused and all the wisdom acquired from reading inspirational books did nothing to change that.

In 2015, at the beginning of the second trimester, a conversation I had with my brother surfaced in my mind. Parfait had made the suggestion that I should write a book on my life experiences. He hinted that an autobiography could be a great source of wisdom and inspiration to many. I really had no idea what the title would be, but as I went through the narrative, the story took on different shapes and forms. I gradually, I moved away from the studies and spent my days at the library in front of my computer screen. I developed a taste for writing, in English, and my memory  helped me to trace my past. My brother got it right. I had an interesting story to share.

A few weeks later, I interrupted my studies to concentrate on publishing my book. I invested all the government grant that I received to invest in the publication of my biography. I enlisted the help of a London-based publisher and eventually, the very first edition of my book was published in May 2015. The title was - How I Won My War.

To this day, I still remember the pride I felt in my heart when I saw and touched the first printed copies. I received a hundred from my publisher and I had to find a way to sell them. I tried out all the digital methods recommended to me. But none of them worked and I was starting to wonder what I would do with the copies. But I knew that I never wanted to work for anyone other than myself ever again.

In the meantime, I attended several seminars on personal development. I found myself in the conference rooms of luxurious hotels crowded with people who, like me, were searching for answers in relation to their own lives. These seminars lasted for days at times and the speakers, usually well-dressed, shared their success stories. It was truly encouraging and inspiring to listen to these warriors of achievement, even though some of the testimonies sounded like fairy tales. Naturally, at the end of each seminar, the speakers always had some merchandise: books or training programs of all kinds.

These meetings were free and motivating. Whenever an opportunity arose, I did not hesitate to attend. However, all of those stories had no impact on my life or even on the sale of my books. Sometimes, I attended parties for single people in some dark places. Desperate men and women gathered there and hoped for a romantic encounter. Women there did not, generally, meet my exceptions. And to be honest, I had nothing to offer a potential mate. I was lost and not in harmony with myself.

One day during one seminar, the speaker, a very charismatic Asian man, emphasised one point that he believed was essential for any progress in life in general and in business in particular: action. As I listened to him, I began to realise how much I had fallen prey of social conformity. I went to these meetings almost every weekend and, like the majority of the people present, I did nothing concrete to put the lessons learned into practice. I had to be proactive.

June 17, 2015 will be forever etched in my memory. That day, I faced fear like never before in my life. The day before, I went to the small supermarket in the neighbourhood to get a cardboard box to carry forty, or so, copies of my book. The idea I had was to go and sell them on the street; a rather unconventional distribution approach . At around 8am,I left the house well-dressed and went to the outskirts of Victoria Train Station in central London. This station has considerable traffic of passengers disembarking and embarking on trains going to and coming from various destinations throughout the United Kingdom and mainland Europe.

I found what I believed to be a suitable place for my trade. I felt knots forming in my belly as I put the box between my trembling legs. I pulled out a few copies and displayed them in the hope that they would be seen by passers-by. A security guard from the station came running and told me to leave the area before being picked up by the council police.

Frightened, I put the copies of my book back into the cardboard box and left. Then I went to sit alone on a nearby public bench to calm the overwhelming fear that had paralysed me to the point of hampering the functioning of my vital organs. After about twenty minutes, I decided to give up and to reflect on another major failure. Feeling defeated I made my way to a bus stop to return home. As I waited for my bus feeling sorry for myself, I saw a young homeless couple sitting not far and looking miserable. I thought to myself that maybe things weren't as bad since I still had a warm flat to go back to unlike them. And that thought made me feel somewhat better.

I went to talk to them and it turn out to be a life changing decision. These young people smiled at me and we started an extremely enriching conversation. Richard, the young man, told me that he hadn't been able to take a bath for eight days; which explained nauseating stench that emanated from him. He and Gloria, his girlfriend, were squatting down the stairs of an abandoned building. The two had no known relatives. Richard told me that their four-year-old daughter was taken away from them and placed with a foster family somewhere in the north of England.

Gloria looked sad. Her dirty and torn clothes did not hide the scars of injuries on the visible parts of her pale and emaciated slim body. She was sitting on a pile of newspaper with a small tin can to receive coins from charitable bystanders. This destitute couple, however, took full responsibility for their miserable life condition. Richard and Gloria were addicted to various narcotics and no drop-in center could keep them: they could not discipline themselves enough to go into rehab.

Their story broke my heart but, in a way, gave me some comfort in my own situation which; compared to theirs, was preferable. I felt very sorry for them. They mainly ate hamburgers that some strangers gave them out of pity. A diet that is poor of nutrients and full of bad fat. After a while, Richard asked me what I was carrying in my box. I explained that I wanted to sell my books in the streets but the police of the London municipality would not let me do that. It was then that Gloria, who was listening intently to us despite her gaze turned elsewhere, interrupted the conversation to give the best advice I have ever received in my life:

"My dear friend, it is always easier to ask for an apology than it is to ask for a permission."

"Wow! - I exclaimed before asking her to explain exactly what she meant.

Once again, I was simply dumbfounded by her reasoning:

"Dear sir," she began before I interrupted her.

"Please simply call me Charly" - I said.

"OK Charly - the police have asked you to leave an area and you want to give up? There are streets all around this station. Just pick a different one and keep doing that until you find one where you will not be disturbed. Besides, when these people tell you to apply for a permission to sell, they know very well that you will never get it. The bureaucracy has destroyed this country. " - concluded this brave young lady.

I was speechless after her brilliant and eloquent pleading . She sounded like a lawyer in court. This skeletal woman had a certain pugnacity about her which did not hide her resentment against a system that evidently crushed her. I asked her how she could remain  so articulate and passionate in her situation. She explained  that her late mother introduced her to books and she was mainly interested in detective novels and everything related to the rights of minorities.

She suggested that I open my box and sell my books next to where they were siting. I moved a few metres away from them to avoid confusion and took up the challenge of setting up my books in full view on the street. Although I still felt the fear, I did it anyway. After about twenty minutes, I made no sales and was beginning to feel discouraged. I started to question the pertinence of that approach of selling.

Suddenly, Richard who had noticed my despondency through my body language, came over to me and patted me on the shoulder. He encouraged me not to give up. He also gave me a very important piece of advice:

"Charly, you have to smile. You have beautiful teeth and you have to use them. You are too rigid. Say hello to everyone and relax your face a bit. You have to put on a show. That's how you will more likely attract the curious."

Just what I needed!

I regained my energy and promised to give him the income from my very first sale. After putting into practice his advice to smile and look a little bit more cheerful, I made my first sale. I was so happy that I started dancing like a little boy. Richard came hopping and cheering for me and with me. We hugged and screamed like olympic medal winners to celebrate this great victory: my first sale on the street.

Then he said a few more encouraging words:

"Charly, I told you everything would be fine. You have to believe in yourself and you will see that you can really do great things and even conquer the world."

This seemed paradoxical to me. I had never been so optimistic. The motivational talks I attended had not affected me as much, nor did all the books I had read. A homeless person, yes my homeless new friend Richard who was about ten years younger than me, was able to boost my self-confidence to a point of no return. I will forever be grateful to him for that. I was born again through that experience.

As promised, I gave him as a reward ten pounds sterling, around seven thousand five hundred CFA Francs, for being my timely motivator. Richard took the money and expressed his gratitude. But he did something that caught me off guard: he went to a close by shop and bought three sandwiches and three small bottles of water. My new friend bought me, his girlfriend and himself some food. After calculating his expenses, I realised that he added his own money to be able to make those purchases. I was stunned by his selflessness. How can such a poor person be so generous? I really couldn't believe it.

The rest of the day went very well. By the end of the fifth hour on that day, I had sold seventeen copies of my book, with a turnover of about two hundred pound sterling. That was about one hundred and fifty thousand CFA francs. Some customers were kind enough to leave me some extra coins that I shared with Gloria and Richard. I parted with this amazing couple at the end of that afternoon. I learned a lot in just a few hours.

The main lesson from this experience is simple but very profound: always treat each person with the respect due to a human being, without discrimination or judgment. If I had not approached this needy couple sitting on the sidewalk, I would not have sold my books

221

and I certainly would not have overcome my fear and my self doubt. And there's more to this: since that sunny day of June 2015, I have sold over four thousand copies of my books on the streets of London in three years. Not bad for a self-published author!

I went every morning to different locations chosen at random to sell. Sometimes I would go to the suburbs, just outside the capital. Business was going relatively well. I would sell an average of eight copies per day. My monthly income was slightly higher than my salary at the Savoy. I spent long hours on my feet and that was causing some back pain.

I went back every now and then to say hello to Richard and Gloria and bring them little gifts and some African food like couscous with peanut sauce that I made at home. They loved it, although sometimes I spiced it a little too much for their taste. One day in December 2015, I went to visit them only to be told that they left. The winter cold had left them with no choice. Having no means of communication, they had gone to another city of England. I never saw them again. I was very saddened, but happy to have met them.

In 2016, I decided to write my story in French and I needed someone I trusted and who was experienced enough to help me in writing this new edition. Thanks to a social network, I found Mr. Joseph Noumo, my French teacher in high school, whom I had lost sight of and contact with for over fifteen years. He agreed to assist me unconditionally.

I travelled to Cameroon twice to meet and discuss the project with him. He spent a lot of his time rereading the first draft, then the second and finally the third.

In 2017, when the book was published by a French publishing company based in Lyon, I returned to Cameroon to show the result to my benefactor. He was very happy and welcomed me in his house like a father would welcome his son. Then I gave him his autographed copy. He held it, looked at it, slipped it between his fingers and passed it carefully from hand to hand and then, expressed his satisfaction. I was very happy to see him so proud. I wish I had had this kind of reaction from my own father. But it was still a consolation for me to have had it from Mr. Noumo who, after all, had encouraged and supported me. He was and remains, as of this day, a person I can turn to in any situation.

To my dear father, I personally delivered a signed copy. He very quickly read the content and was very angry. He expressed his indignation to all of my brothers and sisters, but never said anything to me about it. He grew distant and even more bitter towards me, but never dared to bring up the subject directly. Over time, I understood his attitude. Even though it was not my intention, certain revelations I made in the book struck his sensitivity. It was not, however, some sort of revenge against him. I just wanted to use my past as a source of inspiration for myself first and for my readers. But my father seemed to have had a bad conscience.

Over time, I have come to understand better the man whose name I bear: first the man, then the father. I analysed the conditions in which he grew up. I finally accepted him for who he was. That allowed me to heal from my resentment of him. My complaints had not changed anything and wouldn't change anything. A positive attitude towards him would be more beneficial to my state of mind and inner peace. So a few years ago I took it upon myself to stop complaining and simply to honour him as my father. Because after all, he is and will always be my only father.

My mother received her signed copy from me too and after reading it, she was shocked. She expressed her grief to me and I reassured her. I told her that although the past was difficult, we had to move forward in peace for the next generation. She replied that there would be no next generation if I don't start a family of my own. She reminded me that at my age my father had already had six children.

She was playing her part in encouraging me to get married to start a family. But I had to think about my personal fulfilment first. I decided, very early on, not to get married, or even have children, while I was living outside of Cameroon. I told my mother that the children I would have had in England would have been British and she would not have had the pleasure of watching them grow up and teach them Bati, our mother tongue. To reinforce this argument, I took the examples of my cousins who got married and had children in several countries in the Western world. Many of those children have never set foot in Cameroon and therefore knew little about the culture of their respective parents.

For my mother, this reason was too shallow. All she cared about was that I became a husband and a father. I had another much more personal reason to hold on. Ever since I left my homeland, my deepest desire has always been to return and not have a family until after such a time. In addition, I always wanted to have a wife from Cameroon, even if she is from a different ethnic group. In addition, I have always wanted my children to be in touch with the realities of our country from the time they are born.

My multiple trips between England and Cameroon had no specific purpose. I was a little bored. I was making enough money selling my books and I did not have to worry about money since I had sub-let the largest room in my apartment. The money I collected was enough to cover the monthly rent of the whole flat. So I had to find a solid reason to return and live permanently in Cameroon.

# CHAPTER TWELVE

# Home

---

n 2018, on September 19 to be precise, while I was in Douala for one of my very regular trips, I had a wonderful encounter with someone very special. That morning, I was in a queue boarding a bus to go to Yaoundé where I had a book signing event to attend. I was just about to get onboard when a minor protest started caused by some passengers who had behave in a disrespectful manner. As I was trying to figure out the ins and outs of the quarrel, I saw Martine. Our eyes met and I was immediately struck by her soft gaze and slightly deep dimples. I very calmly got to my seat in the large air-conditioned carrier as the trouble outside subsided. As the vehicle was filling up. Martine got in and took the seat just to my right.

"Lucky me" - I thought.

Although I found her lovely and incredibly attractive, I had no desire to chat her up right then not knowing her situation at that time. Nonetheless, she was a potential client. I got into the habit of selling copies of my book to passengers on the buses, in taxis when moving around in the city. In fact, I sold several copies on the plane during my trips to Cameroon. I have always been an opportunist and I am very proud of it.

After a few basic courtesies, Martine and I started an enriching conversation. I made little jokes to maintain the jovial flow of our conversation; which lasted the entire journey. At the age of thirty-three, Martine had a great life story to tell. She told me that she was a single mother of two daughters aged nine and five. Our conversation focused on personal development, the excesses of our society and the devastating effects of certain religions on some of our compatriots. I was in good company. She revealed to me her love for books. I told her that I was a writer and asked her if she would be interested in a copy of my book. Before she even answered, I used a technique that I have used to great effect in the past. I took out a copy of the book from my bag and handed it to her, saying:

"Martine, I invite you to read the introduction and the first chapter of this book. If you are interested in the story, the book will cost you ten thousand francs. If, on the other hand, the story is not to your liking, I will take the book back and it will cost you nothing at all.

She accepted my offer and, after going through the first few pages, she became a client and handed me a banknote of the agreed amount. I made a special dedication to her in a few words and she thanked me warmly. The trip was long and she read a few paragraphs from time to time along the way. She was asking me questions about certain aspects of my life experiences. When we got to our  destination, we exchanged our contact details and, before leaving, Martine promised to contact me a few days later, to give me her thoughts on my story.

I went to my hotel to get ready for the event of the evening. I sold a few more copies that night and raised a fair amount of money as a result. Then I returned to Douala the next day. My trip back to London was scheduled for the week after. Over the weekend of that week, I waited to hear from Martine as she promised. But she never called or even sent me a text. Without trying to contact her to understand the reason for her silence, I  simply deleted her number from my phone and decided to simply forget about her.

I returned to England to carry on with my business and my life. About two weeks later, I received a message through a virtual communication application from Martine. After trying to reach me in vain, she used my name and found me in the virtual world. In her message to me, she apologised for not keeping to her word. Then, she gave me a glowing review of my book. I responded to her immediately to acknowledge her message and express my gratitude for her positive feedback on my book. I told her also that I was out of town.

As we spoke, Martine explained her situation to me more openly. It turned out that the day she was supposed to call me, she was in court. She had an ongoing lawsuit against the father of her daughters who wanted to take their custody away from her. This explained the sadness I could see in her eyes during our journey together. She was bruised. This legal and family battle cost a lot energy and money. She spent most of her salary on legal fees. I tried as much as I could to comfort her; which she appreciated. Over time, I discovered that we had a lot in common. We spoke every day and it was wonderful. I believed that I found the one special companion that I was waiting for.

But being in England, so far away from her, I knew that the distance would eventually take its toll on the foundation of our relationship. I made no declaration of love to her but I was very hopeful. She had a lot of experience with sharing her life with someone; the father of her children. She spent a few years with him under the same roof. I was approaching my forties and had never lived with anyone. I had no children and this imbalance had to be taken into account. Above all, I had to move back home and be close to her to really have a better idea of what the future held for us.

One day I got home a little earlier than usual and sat down at my computer. I was tired and bored and started to surf on some social media networks. The day had been cold and business had not been good. It was a bit early to call Martine who was still at work at that time of the day. I watched videos indiscriminately and one caught my attention.

It was a video in which the Minister of State for Higher Education was speaking about the computers that his department imported from China for Cameroonian university students. This professor was very eloquent when he spoke in French during televised debates. But in the video that I was watching, he struggled so much to utter a few simple words in English; which resulted in mockery towards him from the whole nation of Cameroon.

I felt sorry for this influential government minister. It must have been rather embarrassing for him to be unable to express himself easily in one of the two official languages of the country in which he was responsible for higher education. I watched this video several times and then saw and opportunity in it. I realised that the Minister must have been out of practice of the English language for many years. I also remembered that over time, I too had forgotten a considerable part of my German vocabulary acquired during my stay in Germany a few years before.

At that moment an idea came to my mind that would start the process of my return home. The project consisted of creating physical and virtual platforms where French-speaking citizens of Cameroon could practice the English language under the supervision of English-speaking moderators from the anglophone regions of the country. I called my younger brother to tell him about it. His opinion was important to me because he had experience on the ground thanks to the profession he had before emigrating to Canada. Parfait went door to door selling insurance and had a better understating of the challenges of local entrepreneurship. He thought that my idea was brilliant.

I told everyone I knew about it and had some useful feedback and recommendation. Martine, to whom I mentioned it, was happy that I was finally returning home permanently. Although I was excited to leave Britain, I had some apprehension. I was turning my back to a very comfortable life in the United Kingdom. I knew that my social reintegration in my country could be more difficult than my integration into Western society. But I had to take the plunge.

I finally left London on September 10, 2019 after eighteen years. I intended to return from time to time, but only for short visits. I wanted to set myself apart through my project. But my family was against my return because Cameroon, at that time, was riddled with social unrests due to political tensions. I had observed other local entrepreneurs who were doing well despite the tensions and that encouraged me to go ahead with my plans.

The house that I had built in Cameroon over a decade before was an asset for what was going to be a new start for me. I turned the living room into an office to work from. I met Martine again and she was very attractive. She was working out of town and I did not have the opportunity to see her as regularly as I would have liked. But we were in constant communication.

After a while, I began to sense a sort of distancing from her. She gradually became fickle in her speech and made promises to me that she broke. She was beginning to show mood swings that I attributed to the tough legal battle between her and her ex-boyfriend. But there was more to it. One day, she confided in me that she was not ready to embark on another love adventure. I was very shocked by her frankness, but I also understood that she wanted to protect her heart by not rushing into a relation so soon after her breakup.

I was very hurt and disappointed. We ended what we had just begun to build. But life had to go on.

I continued to hope that the day would come when I would meet the love of my life: a person with whom I would be more in harmony and who would help me in my many projects; someone that I would also assist in achieving her dreams. But while waiting for this magical moment, I had to continue working and developing my small business. I started advertising my services on social media and reactions came immediately. People contacted me for more information and in early December 2019 I had my first three clients and I was on a roll.

Then came the year 2020.

The new year started and I was full of hope for my business and its expansion. In January, I had more members joining my academy and I recruited some anglophone english teachers to support me. At the same time, the media echoed the ravages of a virus that originated from China and had already claimed thousands of lives in many European countries, especially in Italy. There were daily announcements of deaths. But in Cameroon, people went about their daily lives undisturbed and had a rather casual attitude to what would later become a pandemic.

The world was in a panic mode. African countries in general and Cameroon in particular began to take steps to prevent the spread of the virus. Around mid-March, the barrier measures were announced by the government. One of the safety measures was self-insolation. Gatherings were prohibited. My business took a big hit and I had to stop everything abruptly so as not to not expose my clients to the virus through cross-contamination. I also decided to isolate myself at my house and despite my parents' insistence, I avoided visiting them. At a relatively old age with somewhat failing health, my father was in the vulnerable group.

On April 2, I called home to make sure that everything was okay. It was then that one of my sisters told me that dad was not feeling well and had not eaten properly for days. Suddenly, I told myself that it was surely not alarming since we were used to him having minor fevers. Two days later, he was taken to hospital for tests and It emerged that my dear father had some lacerations in his lungs. The prescribed treatment was followed diligently, but his condition continued to deteriorate.

A thorough examination confirmed what we all feared: Daddy caught the deadly virus. I was shocked and saddened. Despite treatment with herbal teas and other potions from the ancestral medicine, his body weakened to the point where he could no longer feed himself alone. So my mother stepped in to take care of his needs. She fed him and assured that he took his medication. He expressed his infinite gratitude to her for her endeavours.

I took my father to a hospital center where a Catholic missionary said he had found an effective treatment against the coronavirus. There was a huge crowd of patients waiting to be seen by the doctors. It was really heartbreaking to see so many senior citizens suffering from various aches and pains. The distress and anxiety on their faces did nothing to conceal their fear of dying.

My father and I had to wait for long hours. During this period of waiting, I tried as best as I could to keep his mind busy with the political affairs of the country.

Cameroon was in an unprecedented post-election turmoil and every day had its share of twists. Our turn finally came and the doctor took my father's parameters. He asked us some routine questions before giving us the medicine. We returned home and Mom took over to make sure he took it on time and in the right doses.

Over the days and weeks that followed, daddy regained his strength and recovered fully. After being shaken to the point of flirting with the afterlife, he suddenly became as gentle as a lamb. His once deep and, somewhat rough, voice also softened. He changed completely and I recognised the father that I had known in my childhood. My mother was also surprised at this metamorphosis, but saddened by all the time wasted arguing over trivial matters.

I learned a great deal from this situation. Life is a journey that should be an experience of joy and happiness. But one can make it an ordeal through bad choices and actions. Fortunately for my father it was not too late. He still had the time to appease his heart and enjoy the abundance around him. Having experienced extreme poverty as a child, he prioritised money over family harmony. But financial gains would never have effectively replaced the inner peace that could only come from a healthy family environment.

From then on I took great pleasure in talking to him, calling from time to time to check on him directly.

He was quite receptive. Sometimes when I arrived home for a surprised visit, I would find my parents chatting like two adults who valued each other. At forty years of age, I had never seen them so relaxed next to each other. At one point I wanted to thank fate for making my father sick. It was truly paradoxical.

Throughout my adult life, I have always thought that my parents' paths should never have crossed and that they would have lived happier with other spouses. But seeing them so close after the ordeal of my father's illness, I told myself that they really could have seasoned their relationship with a lot of tolerance, if not love. Fortunately it was not too late. My family's harmony was gradually returning.

My business stopped completely as my clients complied with government-mandated barriers measures. It was then that, unwittingly, I had to review my approach. I realised that the meetings in small groups were not at all necessary. By using some digital platforms, we were able to have practice sessions with ease. Then we adopted a new way of delivering our service; which later proved to be efficient and even more profitable.

On the morning of June 18, 2020, I woke up and noticed that I had three missed calls from Jackson. My younger brother had tried to reach me over night in vain. An icy cold wind feeling crossed my whole body and I became afraid. Immediately, I thought that my dad had relapsed and that, surely, he had passed away. My heart pounding, I called Jackson back. In a very reassuring manner, he gave me the news from the night before:

"Charly, it's mom and it's very serious. Around 11:30 p.m., she went to the bathroom and started screaming, complaining of a severe headache. Daddy was the first to get to her. Once she was back in the bedroom, she had a fit of hysteria before collapsing loudly. In doing so, she hit her head violently and defecated on herself, profusely. We are now in a hospital and the doctors have administered sedatives to her. Now she is sleeping. Join us quickly, Daddy has returned home. He was very tired after a long night by her side.

With teary eyes, I got up and sat on my bed. A few minutes later, I got dressed hurriedly. I rushed to he hospital where I found my dear mother pale and asleep. She was snoring intermittently, giving the impression that her breathing was a bit obstructed. I shook her a bit to make sure that she was not completely unconscious. She opened her eyes slightly, then closed them rapidly without saying a word. The nurse told me that the patient's parameters were stable. The results of the samples taken from her would reveal the real extent of her condition. She added that the patient might have had a stroke. But we had to wait for the lab results to be certain.

After this conversation with the doctor, I sat on a bench outside the room that mummy was sharing with three other patients whose conditions seemed just as critical. In the evening, a different nurse approached me and introduced himself before informing me that he had taken over for the night. He held a few sheets of paper in his hands and explained to me all the graphs that were printed on them. From his explanations it emerged that my mother had had a hemorrhagic stroke. Blood had oozed from her brain and was stagnating inside her cranial cavity.

At that time I did not understand the seriousness of this diagnosis. He then informed me that my mother had to be taken to a different and more experienced health center.

Overwhelmed with fear, I asked him a question that surprised him:

"My doctor, will my mother survive?"

He answered tactfully:

"Your mother's brain bleeding makes her situation very serious, but everything will be okay with proper medical attention. She must be taken to the General Hospital where she will be better taken care of. "

After receiving her medical file along with a special written recommendation from the senior doctor, my brother and I took our mother to the General Hospital. We arrived at around 1am and the nurse on duty in the emergency unit welcomed us very courteously. He then asked us to go to the cashier to pay a considerable sum as a deposit. I had used up all the cash I had. The civil servant at the desk was merciless. Although I explained that I did not have the required amount, she insisted on having the full amount before any nurse could look into the patient's file.

Fortunately, my brother had his bank card at hand and was able to withdraw the requested amount from one of the ATMs adjacent to the hospital gate. Once the paperwork was completed, the increasingly agitated patient got the nurse's attention. The nurse was so shocked by what he saw on the graphs in the paperwork that he called his colleagues to come and have a look. One of them shouted:

This is unbelievable!

They all gathered around the papers placed on a lamp attached to the white wall. I stood at a distance by Mum's bed, trying to restrain her agitation and wipe off her mouth. She was spitting impulsively. Worried sick, I looked at them and even though I couldn't hear them, I realised, through their body language, that the news would not be good. We were sent to an air-conditioned room in a quiet corner of this hospital. The hospital staff decided to infused some sedatives into my mother's body to alleviate the pain and to help her sleep. I spent the first sleepless night at the bedside of my ailing mother.

The next day, I drew up a roster for me and my siblings to take turns at our mother's hospital bed. The girls came in the evening and spent the night to bathe the patient in the morning. Jackson and I rotated during the day. Our mother was in a deep coma. Her nutrition consisted of an enriched porridge that the hospital catering service provided. Twice a day, she was fed through a nasal tube using a syringe.

On the fifth day, while I was on call, the neurologist surgeon who I was meeting for the first time took me aside and asked:

"Sir, who is this lady for you?"

"This lady, Doctor, is my mother; I am her first born."

"She looks very young to be your mother. Where is your father? I have something important to tell him," he added.

My reply came without hesitation:

"Doctor, my father is in poor health at the moment. He is recovering from a recent severe illness and is resting at home now. You can talk to me and I will share the information with him later, whatever it is."

Compassionate, the doctor tried to give the information in a language accessible to anyone uninitiated in medical vocabulary:

"Mr. Ngouh, your mother is in an extremely delicate state. We see a lot of patients who, like her, have had a hemorrhagic stroke. Only two out of three survive.

Those who make it usually have lifelong health complication. We will follow the appropriate treatment protocol and we will monitor her blood pressure, blood sugar level and all other. There is, however, something very positive: the patient has not had a fever. That is a good sign."

Scared, I returned to my mother's bedside. But I did not want the fear to spread in the family. I told everyone about the good news that the doctor had shared about our mother not developing any fever and said nothing about the rest of our conversation. For the next few days, I was dying of worry. For hours on end, I watched my immobile mother and thought about all the promises I had made to her that I had broken. I was not yet married and nor did I have any children as she had wished. I had not shown her around the beautiful cities of this world. Her melancholic existence could end at any moment. What would become of me if she died? And why did she have a stroke in the first place?

These questions tortured my conscience and kept my mind awake.

I did some research online to find out the deal causes of stroke as I did ten years earlier, with the autism suffered by the son of Ginette, my host mother in England. I learned that stress can speed up the heart rate, increase blood pressure, and increase blood sugar and cholesterol levels in the blood. Considering the bleakness of her married life and the endless sorrows she had experienced for decades, it was no surprise that my mother became a subject at risk.

By day eight, my mother had still not had a bowel movement and her blood pressure was constantly fluctuating. Always courteous and very attentive, the nurses administered all kinds of laxatives to evacuate the waste which was making her stomach bloated. As a family, we decided to remain positive. We had created a virtual family chat group.

On June 25, at around 11am, mummy had a bowel movement in her diapers for the first time since our arrival at that hospital. I was present and it was my duty to clean her up; which I did with a lot enthusiasm with the help of a nurse. She continued to go to the toilet on herself intermittently over the course of the following days and gradually came out of the coma.

On June 27, the doctors asked us to take our mother home despite her physical weakness. This decision struck us as very strange. But he explained that she was out of danger and that her usual surroundings would help her memory. My mother had lost the use of all of her senses. We reluctantly brought her home. Her eyes were wide open, but she could see nothing. After about two weeks, she began to see more or less clearly, but did not recognise anyone, neither me, her first son, nor my father.

Over the weeks that followed, she regained her strength and, after a few visits to the neurologist and some adjustments in her treatment, she gradually recovered. She needed medical glasses to improve her eyesight. Miraculously, apart from a few stuttering my mother fully recovered without any physical or even psychic infirmity.

During a consultation, the neurologist exclaimed:

"Your mother is almost a miracle; her body has been very receptive to the treatment. that is quite rare."

That was the end of yet another difficult ordeal for me and my family. I will certainly never forget this homecoming: I was happy to have been there when my parents needed me most. This period also allowed me to understand how life hangs by a thread. The fear of losing my parents suddenly made me realise that my excessive attachment to them, especially to my mother, was harmful to my psychological well-being. In reality, she could have left this world, and it would have been pointless for me to live in sadness indefinitely. I also reminded myself that in reality, while it is good to love our family, our duty is first to love ourselves.

The time had come for me to take care of myself, to fulfil my dreams and make myself immortal through my projects.

Thank you for reading my story and therefor, allowing me to invest a part of my life into yours. Please feel free to reach out to me via e-mail: **charlyngouh@gmail.com**.

# The Soldier

# The Boxer

# The Butler

Richard

Gloria

Printed in Poland
by Amazon Fulfillment
Poland Sp. z o.o., Wrocław

19688527R00148